The ESSEN[IIIIII] of

Medieval History

500 to 1450 C.E.
The Middle Ages

Gordon M. Patterson, Ph.D.
Associate Professor of History
Florida Institute of Technology
Melbourne, Florida

Research & Education Association
61 Ethel Road West
Piscataway, New Jersey 08854

THE ESSENTIALS®
OF MEDIEVAL HISTORY
500 to 1450 c.e.
The Middle Ages

Printed in the United States of America

Library of Congress Control Number 00-112091

International Standard Book Number 0-87891-705-5

ESSENTIALS is a registered trademark of
Research & Education Association, Piscataway, New Jersey 08854

What the "Essentials of History" Will Do for You

REA's "Essentials of History" series offers a new approach to the study of history that is a marked departure from what has been available traditionally. Each book in the series has been designed to steer a sensible middle course by including neither too much nor too little information.

Compared with conventional history outlines, the "Essentials of History" offer far more detail, with fuller explanations and interpretations of historical events and developments. Compared with voluminous historical tomes and textbooks, the "Essentials of History" offer a far more concise, less ponderous overview of each of the periods they cover.

The "Essentials of History" are intended primarily to aid students in studying history, doing homework, writing papers, and preparing for exams. The books are organized to provide quick access to information and explanations of the important events, dates, and persons of the period. The books can be used in conjunction with any text. They will save hours of study and preparation time while providing a firm grasp and insightful understanding of the subject matter.

Instructors, too, will find the "Essentials of History" useful. The books can assist in reviewing or modifying course outlines. They also can assist with preparation of exams, as well as serve as an efficient memory refresher.

In sum, the "Essentials of History" will prove to be handy reference sources at all times.

The authors of this series are respected experts in their fields. They present clear, well-reasoned explanations and interpretations of the complex political, social, cultural, economic, and philosophical issues and developments that characterize each era.

In preparing these books REA has made every effort to ensure their accuracy and maximum usefulness. We are confident that each book will prove enjoyable and valuable to its user.

Dr. Max Fogiel, Program Director

About the Author

Gordon M. Patterson is an associate professor of history at the Florida Institute of Technology, where he has taught since 1981. He was a lecturer at the University of Maryland from 1974 until 1981, and an instructor at the University of California at Los Angeles in 1973. He holds two graduate-level degrees from UCLA, as well as a B.S. from Northwestern University.

Dr. Patterson studied abroad in Vienna and at the Universitat Heidelberg, where he was a Fulbright Fellow in 1974–75. He has received three awards from the National Endowment for the Humanities for post-doctoral work at the University of Illinois, the Stanford Dante Institute, and Yale University. He is a member of the German Studies Association and the Dante Society of America.

CONTENTS

NOTE TO READERS

Dates, Names, and Places

Throughout this book dates will be identified as being B.C.E. (Before the Common Epoch) or C.E. (Common Epoch). These expressions cover the same periods as the more familiar B.C. and A.D. without the imposition of a Christian chronological schema. The Christian chronological system was, in fact, devised at the beginning of the medieval period. Before the sixth century of the Common Epoch, most Christians relied on the Roman calendar. In 525 C.E. an obscure monk, Dionysius Exiquus, miscalculated the birth of Jesus and designated that year as the year zero. The actual birth year of Jesus is believed to have been 4 B.C.E. With this erroneous beginning, Dionysius Exiquus numbered events forward (A.D.). The dating of events backward from this temporal midpoint did not begin until the eighteenth century. The Christian calendar was not the only chronological system to appear in the Middle Ages. Within a century of Dionysius, Mohammed's flight to Medina became the beginning point for the Muslim calendar.

The expression "Middle Ages" was first used in the 17th century. This term originated in the desire of Europeans to separate "modern" history from what they considered the long and tedious period which separated their age from the glory of ancient Greece and Rome.

Finally, a word of caution is needed. Precise record keeping disappeared during much of the medieval period. Thus, many of the dates are approximate. Moreover, there are often alternative spellings for proper names translated from foreign languages into English. In such cases, the most common spelling is used.

CHAPTER 1

THE BYZANTINE EMPIRE

1.1 GEOGRAPHY

The area that comprised the Byzantine Empire fluctuated throughout the course of the Empire's thousand-year history. At its greatest extent the Empire spanned the Mediterranean and included Sicily, southern Italy, much of Italy's Adriatic coast, Greece, a sizable part of the Balkans, Anatolia (modern Turkey), and Syria, Palestine, and Egypt.

1.1.1 *The City of Constantinople*

Constantinople was the administrative and economic center of the 1500 cities that constituted the Empire's infrastructure. Founded in 650 B.C.E. by Greek colonists, the city's location at the mouth of the Dardanelles gave it control of access to the Black Sea and the Sea of Marmara. The city's name was changed from Byzantium to Constantinople when Constantine moved his capital to this site in 330 C.E. Constantine expanded the city, ordering the construction of a forum, temples, and an enlarged Hippodrome on the city's seven hills. Constantine's successors continued to lavish favors on the city. Alarmed by

1

the advance of the Germanic tribes, the Emperor Theodosius II (408 – 450 C.E.) ordered his engineers to build a twenty-five foot-high, three-mile-long wall around the city. Theodosius divided his estate between his two sons. One governed the western part of the empire while the other ruled over the wealthier, more stable eastern lands. In 410 C.E. Alaric led the Visigoths when they captured and looted Rome. Constantinople's position as the largest and most secure of the Roman cities was undisputed after the Vandals' sack of Rome in 455 C.E.

1.2 THE CREATION OF THE BYZANTINE EMPIRE

1.2.1 *The Survival of Rome in the East*

During the fourth and fifth centuries the ideal of a unified Roman Empire that joined East and West lived on in spirit if not in fact. The Ostrogoth king, Odoacer, forced the last emperor, Romulus Augustulus (476 C.E.) to abdicate.

1.2.2 *The Sixth Century*

Throughout the sixth century the Eastern emperors worked to recapture the Western provinces. At first these efforts were largely defensive. Between 493 and 526 C.E., Theodoric, king of the Ostrogoths, launched a series of unsuccessful campaigns against Constantinople.

1.2.3 *The Emperor Justinian*

In 527 C.E. Justinian became the Eastern emperor. Justinian and his controversial wife, the steely Theodora, reigned until 565 C.E. Under Justinian's dynamic rule the Eastern Empire recaptured much of the West. Internal difficulties, however, clouded the early years of Justinian's rule. What started as a riot in 532 C.E. in Constantinople proved to be a major test

BARBARIC INVASIONS OF THE ROMAN EMPIRE, c. 400 C.E.

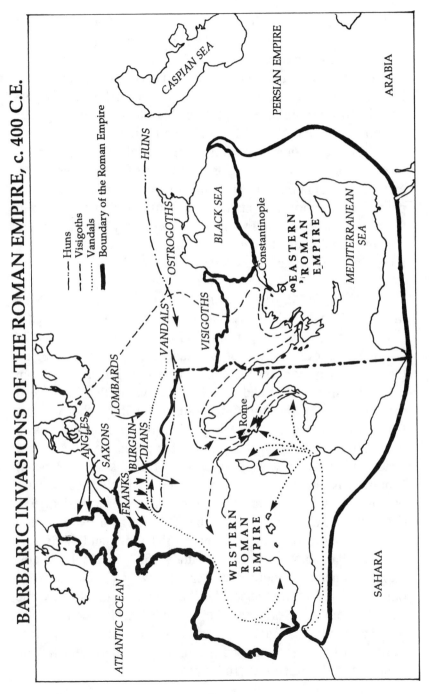

Huns
Visigoths
Vandals
Boundary of the Roman Empire

CASPIAN SEA

PERSIAN EMPIRE

ARABIA

HUNS

OSTROGOTHS

BLACK SEA

Constantinople

EASTERN ROMAN EMPIRE

MEDITERRANEAN SEA

VANDALS

VISIGOTHS

LOMBARDS

ANGLES

SAXONS

FRANKS

BURGUN-DIANS

Rome

WESTERN ROMAN EMPIRE

ATLANTIC OCEAN

SAHARA

3

of his staying power. Sparked by the brutal suppression of a riot by the urban prefect, the Nika riot—*"Nika!"* (*"Let us conquer!"* or *"Let us win!"*) being the rallying cry shouted during the chariot races—marked a rare instance when the city's two main factions, the Greens and the Blues (normally sharply partisan in cheering on their respective charioteers), came together to oppose the autocratic emperor. Swept up in the exuberance of the mob, the rioters soon were in full revolt. They freed their leaders from prison, called for the ouster of government officials, and proclaimed a new emperor, all the while cutting a path of destruction that included burning the Senate House to the ground. The uprising was crushed when a young and gifted general, Belisarius, leader of Justinian's army, corralled the rebels in the Hippodrome and massacred 30,000.

Justinian's Campaigns and Accomplishments. The Nika insurrection, which had posed a grave threat to Justinian's life, not to mention his rule, in the end strengthened his hand to such an extent that he was able to launch a campaign to regain the Western provinces. Justinian chose Belisarius, fresh from his impressively swift and decisive victory, and Narsus to lead the push to dislodge the Ostrogoths from Italy, the Vandals from North Africa, and the Visigoths from Spain. The first step in Justinian's war against the Germanic tribes was to secure a peace along the eastern frontier with the Sassanid (Persian) Empire. Justinian's armies were successful in their early campaigns. Belisarius defeated the Vandals in North Africa (535 C.E.), Sicily, Corsica, and Sardinia. The Visigoths were ousted from their hold on much of Spain (554 C.E.) and Belisarius succeeded in capturing most of Italy (553 C.E.). The campaigns drained the Empire. Disaster came when the plague broke out in 542 C.E. Simultaneously, Slavs and Avars attacked the Empire from the North and the Sassanids broke their accord, waging war in the East. Justinian did not have the resources needed to hold on to his gains. His reign ended with him in control of a shrunken Eastern Empire.

Justinian failed to maintain control of the Western provinces. His Western campaign was the last effort by an Eastern emperor to reunite the Empire. Military disappointments aside, he still left a legacy of accomplishments.

Architecture. Justinian used the devastation occasioned by the Nika revolt as an opportunity to rebuild Constantinople. In 537 C.E. workers completed construction of the Church of Santa Sophia (Holy Wisdom). Santa Sophia was an architectural triumph. Richly appointed, it still stands, serving as an Islamic museum. The dome of the church is 100 feet in diameter and rises 184 feet. Upon the church's completion, Justinian reportedly exclaimed, "O Solomon, I have vanquished you!"

Codification of the Law. At the beginning of his reign Justinian appointed a commission to collect and codify the empire's laws (528 – 534 C.E.). The commission's work became the *Corpus Juris Civilis* (Body of Civil Laws). The *Corpus* was divided into four parts: a *Code* (and ultimately the *Codex Constitutionum*), which streamlined laws that dated back to Hadrian's time; the *Institutes*, a textbook on legal procedure and principles; the *Digest*, a summary of legal opinions; and the *Novels*, which comprised new ordinances decreed by Justinian himself from 534 to 565, following revision of the Codex. The significance of the *Corpus Juris Civilis* was twofold. First, it helped Justinian and his successors centralize power and create an efficient bureaucratic mechanism to administer the Empire. Second, the *Corpus Juris Civilis* became the model on which most of the European states based their legal systems after the twelfth century.

Caesaropapism. As the Byzantine emperor, Justinian exercised supreme political and religious power. This combination of political and religious authority is called caesaropapism. In the West, political power was divided between a number of contesting factions. No Western secular or religious figure exercised autocratic power.

1.3 STAGES IN THE DEVELOPMENT OF THE BYZANTINE EMPIRE

No precise date can be placed on the beginning of the Byzantine Empire. Justinian considered himself Emperor of both the East and West. He spoke Latin and made the defeat of his Western foes his chief objective. By the beginning of the seventh century the Byzantine Empire had come into existence. After 610 C.E. the Emperor in Constantinople spoke Greek and developed a program that was Eastern or "Byzantine" in its orientation.

1.3.1 *The Early Byzantine Empire*

In 610 C.E. Heraclius, the military governor of Carthage, seized control of the Empire and changed the emperor's title (Imperator) to Basileus. Heraclius recognized the impossibility of Justinian's goal of restoring the Empire. He promulgated a new constitution in which Asia Minor was divided into military districts (themes) headed by *strategoi*. In Italy, the Lombards (a Germanic tribe) had pushed the Byzantine forces into an enclave around Ravenna on the Adriatic Coast and into the southernmost parts of Italy and Sicily. The Sassanid Empire in Persia posed a greater threat. Persian armies marched against Constantinople seizing Syria, Palestine, and Egypt. Simultaneously, old foes appeared in the north. The Avars and Slavs attacked Constantinople from the north (626 C.E.). Heraclius confiscated church funds to bribe the Avars and Slavs into accepting a peace settlement. Then, in a daring move, Heraclius left the city to mount its own defense against the Persian onslaught while he marched his army behind the Persian lines. Heraclius defeated the Persian Emperor Chroeses II (battle fought in 628 C.E. near Nineveh).

6

1.3.2 *Islam*

The wars against the Sassanids exhausted the Empire's economic and manpower resources. In 636 C.E. an Islamic army inflicted a major defeat on the Byzantine Empire at Yarmuk. Yarmuk cost the Empire Syria and Palestine. By 652 C.E. Islamic forces had captured the richest of the Empire's provinces. Four years later a Muslim fleet defeated a Byzantine armada and gained control of the Mediterranean (656 C.E.). Between 673 – 678 C.E. Muslim ships blockaded Constantinople. The Byzantine navy succeeded in breaking the siege. In their campaign against the Muslims the Byzantines introduced a new weapon called "Greek Fire." "Greek Fire" was a kind of seaborne flame-thrower constructed around a tube through which a mixture of naphtha, sulfur, and saltpeter was shot at the enemy. The Empire had no sooner broken the blockade than its old enemies, the Bulgars and Avars, attacked from the north. In 679 C.E. the Bulgars crossed the Danube and marched against the city. By 700 C.E. the Empire had shrunk to a fraction of its former size. One hundred and thirty-five years after the reign of Justinian, the Byzantine emperor controlled only southern Italy, Ravenna, a tiny part of the Balkans, and most of Anatolia.

1.3.3 *Leo III*

In 717 C.E. Leo the Isaurian (Syrian), or Leo III, became emperor. During his twenty-four year reign (717 – 741 C.E.) Leo III succeeded in pushing back the Empire's adversaries. In 717 C.E. the Arabs renewed their attack on the city while another Muslim army marched across North Africa and Spain (711 – 719 C.E.). Leo concentrated his resources on protecting the Empire's core. He took steps to reorganize the bureaucracy and administration and succeeded in driving the Muslim troops from Asia Minor (740 C.E.). Leo III's victories gave the Byzantine Empire a two-century respite from further Arab encroachment.

1.3.4 *The Empire and the West*

Throughout the seventh and early eighth centuries there was only minimal relations between the Byzantine Empire and Western Europe. The need to concentrate the Empire's resources on defense and the disarray and inferiority of the West offer a partial explanation for this. These conditions began to change midway though the eighth century. In 732 C.E. Charles Martel stopped the western advance of Islam at Poitiers. Simultaneously, the pope showed a renewed interest in Eastern Christendom. Emperor Leo III provoked a controversy with the Western church when he banned the use of icons in religious services. The pope opposed Leo's proclamation and placed his authority behind the use of images. Relations between East and West worsened between 780 and 802 C.E. In 780 Constantine VI, a ten-year-old, became the Byzantine emperor. Constantine's mother, Irene, acted as regent until 790 C.E. when her son ousted his mother's advisors and seized control. Irene intrigued against her son. Her henchmen blinded Constantine (making him ritually unqualified to be emperor). Irene named herself empress. She ruled from 797 until 802 C.E. Leo III intervened in the controversy when he declared the Eastern throne vacant because a woman could not rule over the Empire. Pope Leo III offered an even greater affront when he unilaterally named Charlemagne "Emperor of the Romans" on Christmas Day in 800 C.E. The practical consequences of Leo III's action were not great. Nevertheless, the naming of a Westerner to head a revitalized Holy Roman Empire signaled the beginning of six centuries of struggle between Western and Eastern Christendom.

1.3.5 *The Macedonian Dynasty*

The emperors who led the Byzantine Empire from 867 C.E. until 1025 C.E. were members of the Macedonian Dynasty. The ninth and tenth centuries were a period of prosperity. Byzantine armies took the offensive, recapturing much of Syria,

Armenia, Cyprus, and Crete. Basil II (976 – 1025 C.E.) smashed the Bulgars and developed friendly relations with Vladimir of Kiev (married Basil's sister) in southern Russia. Vladimir invited Basil (989 C.E.) to send monks into Russia, which led to the conversion of Slavs to Christianity. Trade expanded during these centuries. Reform of the bureaucracy improved life within the Empire's boundaries.

1.3.6   The Decline of the Byzantine Empire

Internal Problems. In the eleventh century the Empire's fortunes changed for the worse. Internally, nobles who had grown wealthy during the period of stability questioned the government's authority. Some nobles transformed their estates into fortresses from which they could disregard the government's decrees. Large landowners paid no taxes (fiscal immunity). The wealthy pursued an aggressive policy directed against the free peasants. This resulted in the seizure of small farms and the near total extinction of small freeholders (feudalization). A manpower shortage forced the emperor to rely on mercenary soldiers. This further exacerbated the Empire's financial difficulties.

External Problems. Externally, the Venetians (after 1082 C.E.) capitalized on their advantage (distance from Muslim powers) to seize many of the Empire's trading posts. In 1054 C.E. the disputes between Western and Eastern churches came to a head, ending in the Great Schism. Finally, a new Islamic people, the Seljuk Turks (named after an early leader), marched out of Central Asia. In 1071 C.E. the Seljuk army defeated the Byzantine army at Manzikert in eastern Anatolia. In the same year the Normans drove the last of the Byzantines out of southern Italy and Sicily.

The Crusades. In 1095 Alexius Comnenus sent a request to Pope Urban II to launch a crusade (holy war) against the infidels. The objective of the First Crusade was to recapture the

Holy Land. Comnenus hoped to use the Crusader army (34,000 Flemish and French troops) to rid the land of Muslim influence. The Crusade succeeded. The Crusaders established small feudal states along the Levantine coast. Comnenus had, however, chosen a perilous course. The First Crusade provoked the Muslims and led to systematic incursions by the "friendly" Crusaders. In 1204 C.E. the Empire's old rival, Venice, used the Fourth Crusade as a pretext for settling the score. The Venetians contracted to move the Crusaders from Europe to the Near East. The Crusaders agreed to pay for their passage by capturing and looting Constantinople. The Crusaders defeated the Byzantine forces in Constantinople in 1204. The Fourth Crusade reached the Holy Land. In 1261 C.E. the Byzantine emperor succeeded in driving the Crusaders out of Constantinople. The revived Byzantine Empire never regained its former power.

The Ottoman Turks and the Empire's Collapse. After the disasters of the thirteenth century the Empire was unable to withstand the attack of Ottoman Turks. The Ottomans had conquered the Seljuk Turks and had obtained control of most of the Byzantine Empire by the beginning of the 15th century. In 1453 the Ottoman emperor, Mohammed II, ordered the final assault on Constantinople. Constantine XI asked Pope Nicholas V to send support. As a condition for his aid, the pope demanded that Constantine acknowledge the pope's primacy. Constantine reportedly declared, "It is better to see in this city the power of the Turkish turban than that of the Latin tiara." The Ottomans put the city under siege. They employed Hungarian engineers to construct cannons that could hurl 1200-pound cannonballs at the city's walls. On May 29, 1453, the city fell.

CHRONOLOGY OF THE EARLY BYZANTINE EMPIRE

325	Council of Nicaea (Nicene Creed)
330	Constantine makes Constantinople his capital
408 – 450	Theodosius II divides Empire between his sons
	Rules from Constantinople
410	Alaric leads Visigoths in looting of Rome
431	2nd Ecumenical Council of Ephesus (Nestorianism a heresy)
451	4th Council of Chalcedon condemns Monophysitism
455	Vandals sack Rome
476	Odoacer (king of Ostrogoths) deposes last Western emperor
493 – 526	Theodoric's (Ostrogoth king) unsuccessful drive against Constantinople
527 – 565	Reign of Justinian
528 – 534	Codification of *Corpus Juris Civilis*
532	Nika Riot leads to civil disorder
535 – 553	Belisarius and Narsus lead armies in the West
537	Santa Sophia completed
542	Plague breaks out in East
568	Lombards win control of northern Italy
610 – 641	Reign of Heraclius
626	Sassanids (Persians) besiege Constantinople
	Avars and Slavs attack the Empire
628	Victory over Persians, Avars, and Slavs
636	Defeat of Byzantines by Arabs at Yarmuk
674 – 678	Arab fleet blockades Constantinople

CHAPTER 2

RELIGION, SOCIETY AND CULTURE IN BYZANTIUM

2.1 CHRISTIANITY IN THE BYZANTINE EMPIRE

2.1.1 *Orthodox Christianity*

Christianity developed a distinctive character under the Byzantine Empire. Early in the Empire's history the Orthodox or Eastern church faced a variety of heresies. Later, the Orthodox church found itself in conflict with its Western brethren over matters involving the Nicene Creed, icons, and papal supremacy. These controversies contributed to the growing rift between the two major branches of Christianity during the Middle Ages. The Great Schism came in 1054 C.E. when the pope excommunicated all of Eastern Christendom, and the Orthodox patriarch of Constantinople excommunicated the Western church.

2.1.2 *Heresy*

Nestorianism and Monophysitism were the two most important heresies to face the early Orthodox church. In 431 C.E. the First Council of Ephesus declared the teachings of Bishop Nestorius a heresy. Nestorius had condemned the growing popularity of the Virgin Mary, arguing that Mary was not "Theotokos" (Mother of God) but rather the "Christokos" (Mother of Christ). The Nestorians claimed that Christ's nature was more human than divine. The Monophysite heresy represented the opposite extreme. These Christians contended that Christ's nature was wholly divine. ("Mono" means one; "physis" means nature.) In 451 C.E., the Council of Chalcedon proclaimed that Christ was both human and divine. The Monophysites were condemned as heretics. The actions of the Council of Ephesus and Chalcedon did not end these heresies. Sizable numbers of Christians continued as Nestorians and Monophysites in the East.

2.1.3 *Disputes with the West*

These Christological disputes (controversies about the nature of Christ) were not the only problems facing the early church. The Council of Nicaea in 325 C.E., and the later church councils, helped define the principal dogmas of the Christian faith. The church councils did not resolve either how these dogmas should be interpreted or the question of who held ultimate authority within Christendom. Initially, the churches that had been founded by the apostles had greater authority than the other Christian communities. The five patriarchs (bishops of Rome, Constantinople, Jerusalem, Antioch, and Alexandria) were equals. By the end of the fifth century the bishop of Rome was pressuring his fellow patriarchs to accept his supremacy. The Germanic invasions and confused state of affairs in the West prevented the Roman pontiff from vigorously pursuing the claim of pre-eminence until the eighth century.

2.1.4 *The Iconoclasts*

The controversy over the use of icons or religious images erupted in the eighth century. Motivated in part by a fear of idolatry and by Islam's condemnation of sacred images, Emperor Leo III issued a proclamation banning icons in 730 C.E. Leo justified his action by references to the Ten Commandments and the life of Christ. Throughout the Byzantine Empire, iconoclasts (image smashers) swept into churches and monasteries and destroyed the religious images that adorned places of worship. The Empire officially pursued a policy of iconoclasm until 843 C.E. Gregory III condemned the iconoclasts, arguing that there was a place for icons within Christianity. Icons could not be worshipped as holy objects in themselves but they could serve a constructive role in educating a universally illiterate laity. Perhaps the most important of the pope's reasons for opposing iconoclasm was the iconoclasts' attack on the cult of saints. The iconoclasts contended that the growing role of saints in Christianity bordered on idolatry. This criticism of the role of saints undercut the pope's argument for his primacy over the other patriarchs since the pope based his claim on his being St. Peter's successor. Until the iconoclasm controversy, relations between the papacy and the Eastern church had been cordial. Iconoclasm led the pope to turn away from the East and seek support from the Frankish king. The pope's naming Charlemagne Holy Roman Emperor in 800 C.E. indicates the rapid deterioration of relations between East and West.

2.1.5 *The Consequences of Iconoclasm*

Iconoclasm flourished for more than a century. Midway through the ninth century iconoclasm's opponents gained the upper hand. They won the readmission of icons and images into the Eastern church. The defeat of iconoclasm had two far-reaching consequences for the Eastern church. First, the Orthodox church adopted a conservative and traditional posture. The

Eastern church avoided innovations lest change reopen the wounds of the iconoclastic controversy. A second consequence was the development of a notion of contemplative piety within Eastern Christianity. Proponents of icons had argued that icons were important because they helped true believers make the transition from the material to the immaterial world. This led to a conception of Christianity which emphasized passivity and mysticism.

2.2   THE GREAT SCHISM

Relations between the pope and the patriarch of Constantinople worsened in the ninth and tenth centuries. In 864 C.E., Boris, the khan of Bulgars, wrote to the pope asking his interpretation of the Nicene Creed. The pope answered that the Holy Ghost proceeds from the father and son. The Orthodox patriarch, Photios (867 C.E.), disagreed and accused the pope of heresy. Photios argued that the Holy Spirit proceeded from God the Father alone. The Photian Schism had religious and political consequences. By 1054 C.E. the relations between East and West had reached a breaking point. The pope sent a representative to negotiate with the patriarch. Discussions broke off with each side excommunicating the other. The split between the Western and Orthodox churches endures to the present with the Eastern church unwilling to accept the pope's primacy or the doctrine of the Virgin's immaculate conception.

2.3   BYZANTINE CIVILIZATION

2.3.1   *Economy: Agriculture, Commerce, and Industry*

The Byzantine Empire retained a strong economy until the 11th century. The free peasantry produced the basis of the Empire's prosperity. After 1025 C.E. large landowners who had gained control of the government's economic policies were able

THE DECLINE OF THE BYZANTINE EMPIRE

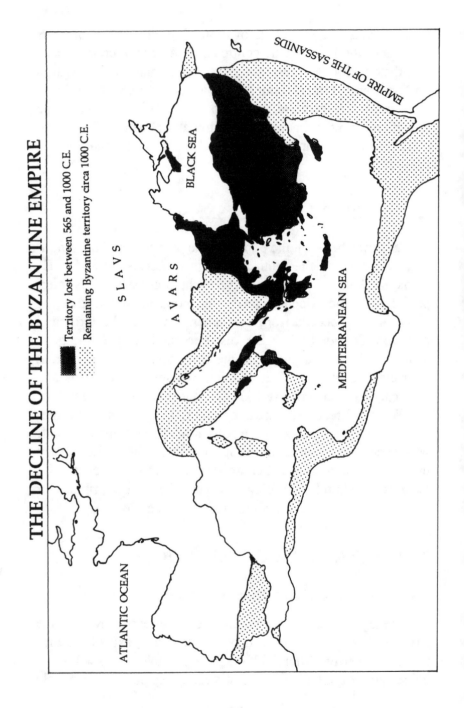

Territory lost between 565 and 1000 C.E.

Remaining Byzantine territory circa 1000 C.E.

ATLANTIC OCEAN

SLAVS

AVARS

BLACK SEA

MEDITERRANEAN SEA

EMPIRE OF THE SASSANIDS

to confiscate the small farmers' land. This ushered in a period of decline which ended in 1453 C.E. when the Ottoman Turks seized control of the Empire. Trade and industry played an important role in the Empire's economy. With a population greater than one million, Constantinople served as the center of a trading network which linked Europe and the Far East. Guilds developed which governed the production of goods.

2.3.2 Education

The Germanic invasion brought an end to the study of Greek and Latin heritage in the West. This was not the case in the East. Byzantine scholars cultivated antiquity, preserving a knowledge of Greek and Latin classics. Some historians have noted that the Byzantine Empire made few original contributions to the classical tradition. Few civilizations would, in fact, do well by this standard. If the Byzantine Empire had not existed, much of the Hellenistic tradition would have been lost. One unique feature of Byzantine civilization was that its educational system was open to women as well as men. Probably the most famous woman intellectual was Anna Comnena. Anna Comnena authored a sophisticated biography of her father, the emperor Alexius Comnenus. The educational system played an important role in developing an efficient bureaucracy. The emperor established schools for future administrators in Athens, Beirut, Alexandria, and other cities.

2.3.3 Art and Architecture

The Byzantine Empire preserved the main tendencies of Greek and Roman art and architecture, while giving them a distinctively Eastern orientation. Byzantine artists distinguished themselves in producing realistic mosaics which decorated the ceilings and walls of most churches. The iconoclasts destroyed virtually all of the works produced in the early Empire. After 843 C.E. new works began to appear. Santa Sophia represents

THE SPREAD OF
CHRISTIANITY, 1000 C.E.

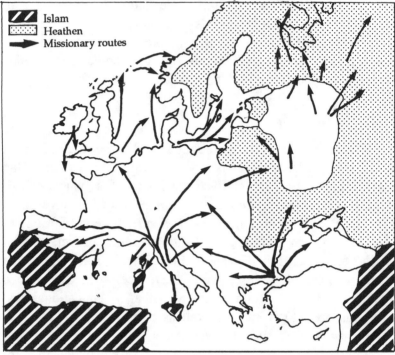

the most brilliant example of the Byzantine Empire's synthesis of the classical and Eastern traditions. Santa Sophia's architect created a structure designed to accentuate God's omnipotence. The church's central feature was the dome which appeared to float above the worshippers' heads.

2.3.4 *The Conversion of the Slavs*

The conversion of the Slavs to Christianity was one of the most important accomplishments of the Byzantine Empire. In the ninth century Saint Cyril and Saint Methodius (ca. 865 C.E.) traveled to Bohemia and Moravia. They developed a new alphabet (Cyrillic) for the Slavic language, as well as translating the Bible for the Slavic peoples. The Cyrillic alphabet is still used in the former Soviet Union and several of the Eastern European countries.

2.4 REASONS FOR THE EMPIRE'S DECLINE

The Empire's stability was tied to its ability to draw on capable leaders, an efficient bureaucracy, and a firm economic base. The Empire began to slide towards collapse when authority fell into the hands of individuals unable to meet the Turkish challenge. The peasants' loss of land undermined the economy. Finally, the Crusades fatally weakened the Empire's resources. The Byzantine Empire that the Ottoman Turks conquered in 1453 C.E. was only a shadow of its former greatness.

CHRONOLOGY OF THE MIDDLE AND LATE BYZANTINE EMPIRE

717 – 802	Isaurian (Syrian) Dynasty
717 – 741	Reign of Emperor Leo III
717 – 718	Arab blockade of Constantinople
	Use of "Greek Fire" to end blockade
730	Leo III bans use of icons
740	Victory over Arabs at Akroinon ends Islamic threat
725 – 843	Iconoclasm Controversy
741 – 775	Reign of Constantine V
751	Fall of Ravenna ends Byzantine rule in Italy
754	Synod of Hereia denounces icon worship as a heresy
	Growing tension between Byzantine emperor and pope over icons
	Byzantine seizure of papal lands in Sicily

797 – 812	Empress Irene deposes Constantine VI
	Pope Urban II declares Eastern throne vacant
800	Urban II crowns Charlemagne Holy Roman Emperor
800 – 1000	High point of Byzantine Empire
812	Michael I concedes title of "Basileus" to Charlemagne
820 – 867	Amoric Dynasty
	Arabs occupy Crete
842 – 867	Michael III sends missionaries to Slavs
863	Expansionist policy in Asia
865	St. Methodius in Moravia
	Bulgars accept Christianity
867	Patriarch Photios breaks with Roman Church
867 – 1056	Macedonian Dynasty
978 – 1015	Vladimir of Kiev accepts Orthodox Christianity
976 – 1025	Basil II (Slayer of the Bulgars)
	Marriage of Basil's sister to Vladimir
1014	Defeat of Bulgars
1025 – 1453	Byzantine Empire in decline
1025 – 1100	Destruction of free peasantry
1045	Capture of Armenia
	Last Eastern expansion of Empire
1054	Great Schism (final break with Western Church)
1059 – 1078	Dukas Dynasty
	Normans, Hungarians, and Seljuk Turks advance
1071	Seljuk Turks defeat Byzantine army at Manzikert
1081 – 1185	Comneni Dynasty
1081 – 1118	Alexius Comnenus
1090	Seljuks attack Constantinople
1095	Alexius requests aid from pope
1096	Beginning of the First Crusade
	Period of Latin Crusader States

1147 – 1149	Second Crusade
1148	Anna Comnena's biography of her father
1189 – 1192	Third Crusade
1185 – 1204	Angeli Dynasty
1204	Fourth Crusade and conquest of Constantinople
1261	Byzantine forces regain control of Constantinople
1301	Beginning of rise of the Ottoman Turks
1337	Ottomans seize Nicomedia
1354	Ottomans seize Gallipoli
1389	Ottomans seize the Balkans
1451 – 1481	Mohammed II (The Conqueror)
1453	Constantinople falls

CHAPTER 3

ISLAMIC CIVILIZATION IN THE MIDDLE AGES

3.1 GEOGRAPHY AND THE PRE-ISLAMIC ARABS

Arabia (the geographical origin of Islam) consists of the desert and steppe lands which extend northward from the tip of Yemen through the Syrian desert, to the settled agricultural lands of Anatolia (central Turkey) and Armenia. Arabia extends eastward to the Tigris and Euphrates Rivers and westward to the Red Sea.

3.1.1 *Early Arab History*

The Nabatean Arabs defeated the Romans in 106 C.E. They established a trading center in Petra (modern Jordan) which gave them control of the trans-Jordanian trade routes. To the north other Arabs captured Palmyra and dominated the northern trade routes linking central Asia to the Mediterranean coast.

3.1.2 *Economic Life: Pastoralism and Commerce*

The early Arabs were pastoralists who tended herds of sheep, goats, and camels. The region's harshness led to wars over water and pastures. The tribes regularly extracted taxes from settled peoples. Not all of the Arabs were nomadic pastoralists. Many lived in cities which grew up around oases, such as Yathrib (Medina), or developed agricultural settlements as in parts of Yemen. The Arabs dominated the trading network which connected East and West. Two different kinds of trade goods passed across Arabia: luxury items, such as perfume and spices, which originated in India and China; and local goods, such as the frankincense and myrrh used in funerals, which were produced in Arabia and shipped to Rome. Arab traders organized a network of trading stations to move goods from India and China. It was impossible to send armed parties to protect caravans as they passed across the Arabian desert. Instead, the great Arab trading families developed a series of way stations (caravansary) and agreements between different tribes which allowed the caravans to pass safely.

3.1.3 *Social Organization*

The clan (extended family) was the basis of a kinship system that knitted the Arab tribes together. The Arabic language played an important role in fostering a pan-Arab sensibility. There were many dialects. Commerce fostered the formation of a common language. Individuals identified with the group to which they belonged. Leadership among the Arabs was not based on the accumulation of wealth in gold. Positions of power fell to those with reputations for wisdom and generosity.

3.1.4 *The Pre-Islamic Religion*

In the first centuries of the Common Epoch, most Arabs (in inner Arabia) were pagans who worshipped a variety of local

23

deities. Arabs who lived in Byzantine cities and in Spain were almost exclusively Christian. In Mecca, the local Arab religion contributed to the city's commercial character. Mecca grew up around a *haram* (a neutral ground where rival traders would meet to exchange goods). Harams were located at sacred places where a ban was placed on theft and murder. A holy man often served as arbitrator in the disputes between traders who had assembled at a haram. Mecca developed around a haram whose center was the *Kaaba*. The Kaaba was a building which surrounded a black stone and a collection of religious idols. The Quraysh tribe controlled Mecca and the trade routes passing by the city.

3.2 THE LIFE OF MOHAMMED

3.2.1 *Youth and Early Manhood*

Mohammed was born into the Quraysh tribe in 570 C.E. His father perished before his birth. His grandfather and mother (Amina) raised him until his mother died when he was six. His grandfather's death two years later left him an orphan. Mohammed's uncle, Abut Talib, took the boy. This was a period of growth and prosperity in Mecca. Abu Talib introduced his nephew to commerce. He may have taken Mohammed on trading journeys to Syria where Mohammed would have been exposed to Christianity and the Byzantine Empire. In the late sixth century, trade was the avenue that led to success. Mohammed was intelligent and ambitious. In his early twenties he became the manager of the property of a wealthy Quraysh widow (Khadija). Marriage followed.

3.2.2 *From Revelation to Hegira*

Around 610 C.E., when Mohammed was forty years old, he received a revelation from the archangel Gabriel. Gabriel revealed to Mohammed that there was one God (*Allah* is the

Arabic word for God) and that Mohammed was his prophet. Mohammed's successors later collected these revelations in the Koran (Quran). Mohammed launched his public ministry by preaching to his brethren. His wife, Khadija, was his first convert. At first only Ali (his sixteen year old cousin), Abu Bakr (a prosperous merchant) and one of Mohammed's former slaves accepted Mohammed's teachings. The leaders of the Quraysh family did not oppose Mohammed at the beginning of his ministry. They became alarmed when Mohammed attacked the haram's idols. During this period Mohammed toyed with the idea of tolerating four of the pagan goddesses. Some scholars have interpreted these verses as Mohammed's attempt to make a conciliatory gesture. Mohammed repudiated these "satanic verses" and reaffirmed that there was only one God. The Quraysh elders judged Mohammed a troublemaker and ordered a boycott of Mohammed's supporters in the Hashim clan. In 614 C.E. Khadija died. Mohammed's followers grew during the next eight years. The leaders of the Quraysh ordered Mohammed's assassination. On September 24, 622 C.E. (the Islamic calendar dates from this moment) Mohammed and seventy of his followers (called the "Muhajirun" or emigrants) fled from Mecca to Medina. The Ansar (people in Medina who had converted to Islam) welcomed Mohammed. The Muhajirun and Ansar formed a community. This body was called the Umma.

3.2.3 Victory Over Mecca

Mohammed realized that the survival of the faith depended on who controlled Mecca. Mohammed's followers launched raids against Quraysh caravans soon after their arrival in Medina. In 624 C.E. Mohammed won a critical victory over his opponents. Three years later, the Meccans sent a force of 10,000 men against the prophet. Mohammed's troops were outnumbered three to one. The Quraysh put Medina under siege. After three weeks the Meccans retreated. This proved to be a turning point. Three years later Mohammed marched into Mecca (630 C.E.). Mohammed died on June 8, 632 C.E.

3.3   THE TEACHINGS OF ISLAM

3.3.1   *The Five Pillars*

Islam (the word means "submission") is based on the belief that there is one God and that Mohammed is his prophet. All of Mohammed's teachings derive from this tenet. The Sharia (code of law and theology) outlines five pillars of faith that every Muslim (one who submits to Allah) must endorse. First, Muslims must proclaim that there is one God, that God is Allah, and that Mohammed is his prophet. Second, every Muslim is obliged to pray five times each day (sunrise, noon, midafternoon, sunset, and nightfall). A muezzin calls the faithful from a minaret (tower) at the mosque. Initially, Mohammed commanded his followers to pray facing the direction of Jerusalem. Later he altered this and ordered them to direct their prayers towards Mecca. Third, every Muslim must perform charitable acts. Offerings must be given to the poor. Fourth, Muslims fast during the holy month of Ramadan between sunrise and sunset. Ramadan concludes with a three-day celebration that commemorates Mohammed's "Night of Power." Finally, Mohammed directed his followers to make a *hajj* (pilgrimage to Mecca) at least once during their lives. Those too poor or unfit for the journey may gain a dispensation from this obligation by contributing to another's pilgrim journey.

3.3.2   *The Koran (Quran)*

The Koran (Quran) contains Mohammed's sacred teachings. It consists of 114 suras (verses). The prophet's followers collected (644 – 656 C.E.) the 114 suras that compose the Koran nearly twenty years after Mohammed's death. The Koran is not arranged in either a thematic or chronological manner. The length of the sura determines its position in the Koran. The longest suras come first and the shortest last. After Mohammed's death questions arose which were not specifically addressed in the Koran. A body of teachings called the Sunna (customs) developed. The Sunna presented episodes from Mohammed's life. Islam differs from Christianity in that there is no provision for an organized priesthood. Mullahs (teachers) occupy positions of authority because of their knowledge of the Koran and the Sunna. Islam did not develop a hierarchical system comparable to either Eastern or Western Christianity.

3.3.3 *Moral and Social Character of Islam*

Islam represents a way of life. Mohammed demanded that the faithful show their commitment to Allah in every part of their existence. The Koran prohibits alcohol and gambling as well as eating "the flesh of animals that die a natural death, blood, and pig's meat." The faithful were obliged to protect widows and orphans. Polygamy was tolerated (maximum of four wives) but husbands could not divorce their wives without grounds. Mohammed's teachings rest on a conception of God that holds men and women accountable for their actions. On Judgment Day, Allah will reward the faithful with a paradise filled with eternal pleasure. Infidels and apostates will be damned for eternity to "chains and Blazing Fire."

3.3.4 *Islam, Judaism, and Christianity*

Islam shares certain tenets with Judaism and Christianity. Both Judaism and Islam proclaim a strict monotheism. Islam differs from Judaism in its being a creed open to all. In this it resembles Christianity. Not being an Arab poses no barrier to becoming a Muslim. Anyone who accepts Allah, recognizes Mohammed as the prophet, and lives according to the Koran is a Muslim. Allah is identical with the God in the Hebrew Scriptures and the New Testament.

CHRONOLOGY OF THE LIFE
OF THE PROPHET

570 – 632	Mohammed
610	Revelation on Mt. Hira
June 15, 622	Hegira (Flight) to Medina
625 – 626	Expulsion of Jews from Medina when they refused to accept Islam
November 1, 630	Mohammed's return to Mecca
June 8, 632	Death of the prophet

CHAPTER 4

THE EXPANSION OF ISLAM

4.1 ISLAM AFTER THE DEATH OF THE PROPHET

Mohammed's death created a leadership crisis which was soon transformed into a political struggle. At his death, the leadership of the Umma (Muslim community) was divided between the Muhajirun (emigrants who accompanied Mohammed to Medina) and the Ansar (who welcomed the prophet in Medina). Between 632 and 1258 C.E. there were three groups of caliphs (successors to the prophet). The first group ("the rightly guided caliphs") consisted of the first four caliphs. The Omayyad Dynasty (661 – 756 C.E.) made up the second. The Abbasid Dynasty (750 – 1258 C.E.) supplied the last.

4.1.1 *The First Four Caliphs*

Most agreed that Mohammed's father-in-law, Abu Bakr, should serve as caliph (caliph or "khalifa" means successor to the prophet). Abu Bakr faced a number of challenges in the two years he served as caliph before his death in 634 C.E. Some tribes refused to accept his authority. They argued that they had bound themselves to Mohammed and not to Islam. Abu Bakr organized an army which defeated his opponents. When he died the Muslims controlled all of Arabia. Before his death, he selected Omar as his successor.

Omar established the basis of the Islamic Empire between 634 and 642 C.E. He chose Khalid ibn-al-Walid (called the Sword of Islam) to lead the Muslim army. In 635 C.E., Khalid's troops defeated a larger Byzantine army. Jerusalem fell in 637 C.E. Another army marched against the Persians. The Sassinids collapsed in 644 C.E. In 639 – 40 C.E., Arab forces struck out across the Sinai and captured Egypt and much of North Africa. A Christian slave assassinated Omar in 644 C.E. Ali (one of the original converts and the husband of Mohammed's daughter, Fatima) and Othman (a leader of the Meccan faction) were the principal candidates for caliph. Ali refused to promise to adhere to Omar's pro-Mecca policies and the Umma named Othman caliph. Traditionally, Othman's caliphship is divided into two parts: six good years which were followed by six bad years. During the first period scholars compiled the Koran and Islam continued to expand eastward into Iraq and Iran. Discontent with Othman's policies crystallized in the second period. Othman's efforts to acquire more power angered many of his former supporters. Others felt that the caliph should belong to Mohammed's family. In 656 C.E. Othman was murdered. The leaders of the Umma elected Ali caliph. Controversy marked Ali's five years as caliph. Othman's cousin, the governor of Syria (Muawiyah), opposed Ali's appointment. Ali enraged Othman's followers when he refused to punish his predecessor's murderers. Ali was assassinated in 661 C.E.

4.1.2 *The Omayyad Caliphs*

The Umma's leaders chose Ali's Syrian opponent, Muawiyah, as his successor. Muawiyah founded the Omayyad Dynasty. Based in Damascus, the Omayyads governed as ca-

THE EXPANSION OF ISLAM

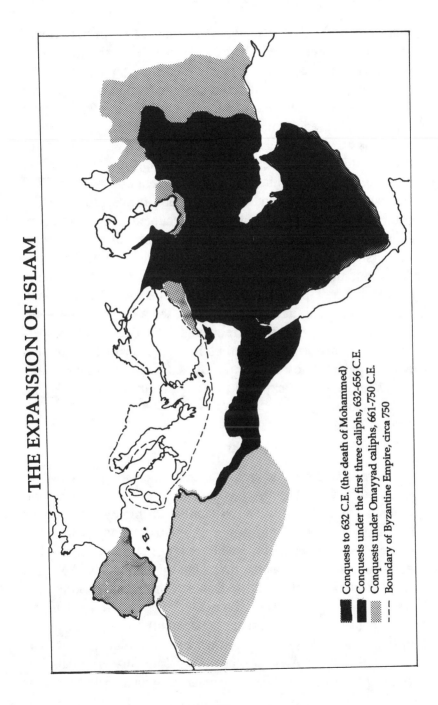

Conquests to 632 C.E. (the death of Mohammed)

Conquests under the first three caliphs, 632-656 C.E.

Conquests under Omayyad caliphs, 661-750 C.E.

Boundary of Byzantine Empire, circa 750

liphs until 750 C.E. Ali's supporters broke from the majority of the Islamic community. They called themselves Shiites ("shi" is Arabic for "follower"). They argued that Ali's descendants were Mohammed's true successors. Shiites believed that at some future time an Iman (one of Mohammed's direct descendants) would appear and bring victory to Shiism. The majority of Muslims called themselves Sunnites (from the word "sunna" or oral traditions about the prophet). The dispute between Shiites and Sunnites did not interfere with the spread of Islam. By 720 C.E. an Islamic army had captured Spain. In the 720's Muslim soldiers crossed the Pyrenees and occupied part of southern France. In 732 C.E. Charles Martel stopped their advance at Poitiers and Tours. Muslim armies continued to advance in the East until they penetrated into India and China. The Islamic armies did not proselytize conquered peoples. Nevertheless, Islam's universal creed and its successes attracted many converts. The Omayyad caliphs reigned during a period of prosperity. They transformed Damascus into a center of learning and commerce. The closeness of the Byzantine Empire insured that the Omayyads were exposed to the main currents of the Hellenistic tradition.

4.1.3 *The Abbasid Caliphs*

A revolt broke out in Iraq against the Omayyads in 747 C.E. In 750 C.E. Abu-l-Abbas defeated an Omayyad army and ordered the caliph's execution along with ninety members of his family. One Omayyad prince (Abd-ar-Rahman) managed to escape to Spain, where he established himself as caliph of Cordoba. Abu-l-Abbas was the first Abbasid caliph. The Abbasids ruled from 750 until 1258 C.E. when the Mongols killed the last Abbasid caliph. The Abbasid caliphs transformed, Islam. They constructed a new capital (Baghdad) on the Tigris River in Iraq. This represented more than a geographical change. The Abbasids treated Arab and non-Arab Muslims as equals. Increasingly, Islam assumed a Persian character. The two most famous Abbasid caliphs were: Harun-al Rashid (786 – 809 C.E.) and Al-Maman (813 – 833 C.E.). Harun-al-Rashid is known because of the collection of stories called the *Thousand and One Arabian Nights*. Historians remember Al-Maman because of his patronage of the arts and sciences. During the late tenth and early eleventh centuries the Islamic Empire began to disintegrate. The Omayyad caliphs of Cordoba controlled Spain. Between 973 and 1171 C.E. the Fatamids (branch of Shiites) governed Egypt. In 1055 C.E. the Seljuk Turks captured Baghdad. They allowed the Abbasids to rule as their figureheads. Real power passed to the Turkish Sultan. Genghis Khan (1167 – 1227 C.E.) led the first Mongol wave against the Abbasids. In 1258 C.E. the Mongols seized Baghdad and murdered the last Abbasid caliph.

4.2   MATERIAL CULTURE

4.2.1   *Economy and Society*

Islamic civilization was dynamic and cosmopolitan from its inception in the seventh century until the sixteenth century. Its material and intellectual accomplishments eclipsed developments in the West in virtually every field. This success was rooted in its economic prosperity. The economic life of the Islamic peoples centered on commerce and industry. Mohammed was not a nomadic, desert Arab. His family was one of the powerful trading clans whose business dealings spanned Arabia. Islam encouraged trade. Geography contributed to this tendency. The Arab merchants controlled the trade routes that linked the continents of Africa, Asia, and Europe. The Muslims founded cities such as Cairo and Baghdad. Industries developed in these cities. Damascus was famous for its steel and "damask" (woven silk); Toledo for swords; Mosul (Syria) for cotton; Baghdad for glassware, pottery, and silk; and Morocco for leather. Caravans crisscrossed the Muslim world carrying goods from China in the East to Europe in the West. These commercial dealings encouraged Islam's cosmopolitan outlook. The frequent dealings with infidels encouraged tolerance. Muslim authorities allowed Christians and Jews to practice their religions. Infidels (Christians and Jews) paid a tax for this privilege.

4.2.2 *Women in Islam*

In one area, however, Islamic society manifested a striking intolerance. Women were treated as property. The Koran sanctioned polygamy, but placed a limit of four on the number of wives a man could take. Wealthy Muslims employed eunuchs to guard their harems.

4.3 SCIENCE AND PHILOSOPHY

Throughout the Islamic civilization's history, there has been a tension between those who devoted themselves to preserving Islam's purity and those who wished to explore new avenues of thought in the secular world. The medieval Islamic civilization exhibited an astonishing dexterity in balancing these rival intellectual traditions. One reason for this is that Mohammed did not authorize an organized priesthood. In time, two different kinds of religious authorities appeared. One group, the Ulama, consisted of individuals who devoted their lives to the careful study of the Muslim sciences and religion. The Ulama were experts on Islamic law and the application of the Koran to everyday life. The Sufis offered an alternative to the Ulama. The Sufis resembled Christian monks in the medieval period in their commitment to contemplation. The Sufis, however, did not withdraw from the world. They married and lived in brotherhoods. Alongside the Ulama and Sufis there were other individuals who devoted their lives to studying science and philosophy. Called Faylasufs (after the Greek "philosophia," which they cultivated), these individuals succeeded in preserving and enhancing the Hellenistic tradition.

4.3.1 Mathematics

The Faylasufs laid the foundation for the modern study of mathematics. Trade brought Muslim mathematicians into contact with the Hindu decimal system of notation. Arabic numerals are, in fact, an adaptation of the Indian system. In 850 C.E. Khwarizmi published a mathematical treatise describing "al-Jabr" (origin of the word "algebra"). Another mathematician, Omar Khayyam (better known as a poet), pioneered the field of analytical geometry.

4.3.2 Astronomy and Geography

Islamic scientists focused on practical problems. This was particularly true in astronomy. The Koran required Muslims to pray five times a day. This placed a premium on the accurate calculation of sunrise, noon, and sunset. Equally, the Koranic requirement that the faithful direct their prayers towards Mecca led to advances in geography. The geographer al-Idrisi was the first person to place his maps on a sphere.

4.3.3 Physics and Chemistry

In physics and chemistry the Faylasufs made important advances. Historians consider Muhammed ibon al-Haitham (965 – 1039 C.E.), known in Medieval Europe as "Alhazen," to be the "father of optics." Aristotle's belief that there were four primary elements shaped the development of Islamic physics and chemistry.

4.3.4 Medicine

Islamic scientists made their greatest advances in medicine. The Abbasid caliph, Harun-al-Rashid, founded the first Muslim hospital in Baghdad, in the eighth century. Hospitals spread throughout the Islamic world. Patients were divided into wards. Each hospital kept its own pharmacy. Medical schools used the hospitals as part of their teaching facilities. The Persian Rhases

(860 – 925 C.E.) and the Arab Faylasuf Avicenna (980 – 1057 C.E.) were the two greatest Islamic medical researchers. Scholars credit Rhases with more than two hundred works. Avicenna produced an encyclopedic *Canon of Medicine*. He identified tuberculosis as a contagious disease and argued that contaminated water and soil caused many illnesses.

4.3.5 *Philosophy*

The major accomplishment of the Faylasufs was the preservation of the Greek philosophical tradition. When knowledge of Greek philosophy had disappeared in the West, Islamic philosophers carried on the traditions of Plato and Aristotle. As a student, Avicenna devoted himself to Aristotle. The philosopher Averroes (1126 – 1198 C.E.) provided a commentary on Aristotle's work that served as a guide for Western scholars. Averroes lived in Cordoba. This made his translations and commentaries accessible to Western scholars who began to show a renewed interest in antiquity during the thirteenth century.

4.4 LITERATURE

The Koran exercised a profound influence on Islamic literature. Muslims consider the Koran to be literally God's sacred word. That is why every Muslim is obligated to learn to read the Koran in Arabic. Muslim writers produced secular poetry and prose. In *The Rubaiyat* Omar Khayyam drew on Greek, Arab, Persian, and Egyptian sources in creating a sensual and worldly poetic work ("a jug of wine, a loaf of bread, and thou"). Ibn Khaldun's seven-volume *Universal History* was the most famous Islamic historical work.

4.5   ART AND ARCHITECTURE

The Koran prohibits the representation of human and natural forms. This gave a distinctive quality to Islamic art and architecture. Muslim artists cultivated a geometrical approach to art. This is especially apparent in the ornate calligraphy (beautiful handwriting) used to produce copies of the Koran and other Arabic texts. The Persian and Byzantine Empires influenced Muslim architecture. Some of the characteristic features of Islamic architecture include: the minaret, horseshoe arches, bulbous domes, and twisted columns. The Dome of the Rock (691 C.E.) was the first major Islamic architectural achievement outside Arabia. The caliph ordered that the Omayyad Mosque in Damascus be built on the site of what was successively a Greek, then Roman temple, then Christian church. The architects used the Roman walls and watchtowers in the mosque's construction.

4.6.   THE CONTRIBUTIONS OF ISLAMIC CIVILIZATION

Medieval Islamic culture left a lasting imprint on the development of civilization. Words tell much of the story. The terms zenith, nadir, zero, and the names of stars like Alderan and Betelgeuse, along with amalgam, alembic, alchemy, alkali, soda, and syrup all have their origin in Arabic. While Western Europe was languishing in the wake of the Germanic invasions, the Islamic peoples were vibrant and creative. It is difficult to overstate the West's debt to the medieval Islamic world.

CHRONOLOGY OF
THE EXPANSION OF ISLAM

632 – 634	Abu Bakr Caliph
634 – 644	Omar "Ruler of the Faithful" Caliph
635	Syria conquered
638	Jerusalem falls
636 – 642	Persia conquered
642	Egypt conquered
644 – 656	Othman Caliph continues program of conquest
	Koran collected during this period
656 – 661	Ali Caliph
	Struggle between rival factions
661	Ali murdered
661 – 750	Omayyad Dynasty (Damascus)
667	Expansion into Byzantine Empire
680 – 683	Yazidi defeats Ali's son, Husain, at Kerbela
705 – 715	Walid I; High point of Omayyad Dynasty
711	Conquest of Indus Valley; Tariq crosses Straits of Gibraltar into Spain
723 – 733	Defeat at Tours and Poitiers halts Arab advance in West
750	Fall of Omayyad Caliphs
756	Emirate of Omayyads at Cordoba
750 – 1258	Abbasid Dynasty (Baghdad)
754 – 775	al-Mansur "the Victorious," real founder of Abbasid Dynasty, adopts Persian and Byzantine government models
762	Capital moved to Baghdad; Persians predominate
786 – 809	Harun al-Rashid; High point of Abbasids *One Thousand and One Arabian Nights*
788	Idrisid Dynasty in Morocco (Fez)
940 – 1256	Erosion of Abbasid's authority

969 – 1171	Fatamid Dynasty in Egypt
1055	Seljuk Turks capture Baghdad and rule as Sultans
	Abbasid caliph is figurehead
1167 – 1227	Genghis Khan; First Mongol Empire
1205 – 1225	Conquest of China
1256	Mongol drive into Persia
1258	Mongols capture Baghdad
	End of Abbasid Dynasty

CHAPTER 5

THE EARLY MIDDLE AGES

5.1 OUTLINE OF THE HISTORY OF THE EARLY MIDDLE AGES

5.1.1 *Geography*

The Mediterranean served as the geographical center for civilization in antiquity. The Germanic invasions of the fourth and fifth centuries opened the European phase of Western history. From a geographer's perspective Europe is an extension of Asia. Between 486 C.E. and 1050 C.E. Europe acquired a distinctive identity. Physically, Europe is comprised of three different regions: those lands bordering on the Mediterranean; the plains of Central and Eastern Europe; and the lands west of the Alps. It is difficult to identify precise boundaries for the region. Europe extends from the Mediterranean to the Baltic and from England and Ireland to the Black Sea and Ural Mountains in the East. The region enjoys a temperate climate. With the exception of some areas in the south, Europe receives sufficient rainfall. At the beginning of the Middle Ages, Europe was heavily forested with probably less than 10% of the land under cultivation. Finally, Europe possesses a number of navigable rivers.

5.1.2 *Europe in Antiquity*

Reports from Roman historians and modern archaeological research demonstrate that much of Europe was occupied by Germanic tribes in antiquity. The Germanic tribes share a common Indo-European origin. The Northern Germanic tribes settled in Scandinavia. The Vikings and Norsemen were their descendants. The Eastern Germanic tribes (Vandals, Burgundians, and Goths) are closely related to the Northern tribes. They settled east of the Elbe River. The Saxons and Lombards dominated the Western Germanic Tribes. Pliny, the Roman naturalist and historian, mentioned the Germanic tribes' presence in his *Natural History* in 95 B.C.E. The tribes lived in small groups with the clan serving as the basis of social organization. The Slavs were the predominant people in Eastern Europe and Russia. Finally, mounted nomadic people moved across the steppes which begin in Russia and run to the Yellow Sea. The Huns were the first of these nomadic people to push across Central Asia and invade Europe. In 375 C.E. they overran the Ostrogoths (Eastern Germans), and then returned to their homeland. Their advance pushed the Eastern Germanic tribes westward and into conflict with the Roman Empire. In 378 C.E. the Visigoths defeated a Roman army in the Battle of Adrianople. In 401 Alaric led the Visigoths across the Alps into Italy. Nine years later Alaric's army looted Rome. The Visigoths' advance drove another Germanic Tribe, the Vandals, into Spain. The Vandals occupied Spain (409 C.E.) and crossed the Straits of Gibraltar and conquered North Africa (429 C.E.). In 455 C.E. the Vandals sacked Rome. While these events were occurring in the West, Attila was leading a second wave of Huns out of Central Asia (441 – 453 C.E.). Odoacer, the king of the Ostrogoths, moved his people westward. In 476 C.E. he compelled the boy emperor, Romulus Augustulus, to abdicate. This was the end of the Western Roman Empire. Seventeen years later Odoacer was overthrown by Theodoric (493 – 553 C.E.).

5.1.3 *The Kingdom of the Franks*

The Frankish kingdom was the most important of the Germanic states during the early Middle Ages. In the fourth and fifth centuries the Franks gradually pushed the Romans out of Gaul. Clovis (482 – 511 C.E.) defeated the last remnants of the Roman forces (486 C.E.) and made himself king of the Franks. In 493 C.E. Clovis married a Christian woman named Clothile. Three years later he converted to Christianity after promising to become a Christian if he was successful in defeating a rival Germanic tribe which had contested his claim to Gaul. By 500 C.E. Clovis had subdued his foes. He named himself king of the Franks and established the Merovingian Dynasty. The term Merovingian originated in one of Clovis's ancestors, Merovech, who had helped the Romans defeat Attila in 451 C.E., in the Battle of Chalons.

The Frankish "Do-Nothing" Kings. Clovis had a talent for mingling cunning with brutality. His successors lacked this ability. The Merovingian kings were known as the "Do-Nothing" kings. An official called the Mayor of the Palace held real power. This position passed from father to son. By the beginning of the eighth century the Mayors of the Palace governed the Franks. In 732 C.E., one of the Mayors, Charles Martel (Martel means "the Hammer") defeated an advance party of Muslim warriors at Poitiers. Martel's son, Pepin (751 – 768 C.E.), was not content with being Mayor of the Palace. Pepin persuaded Pope Zachary to depose the Merovingian monarch and crown him king of the Franks. Pepin had earned the pope's gratitude through his successful campaign against the Lombards who controlled northern Italy and who posed a threat to

THE GROWING SEASON IN EUROPE

Beginning in June
Beginning in May
Beginning in April

the pope. Pepin found another ecclesiastical ally in Saint Boniface. Pepin agreed to support Boniface in his effort to Christianize the German tribes east of the Rhine and Elbe Rivers in return for Boniface's intercession with the pope.

5.1.4 *Charlemagne*

When Pepin died, his son, Charles, succeeded him as King Charles (768 – 814 C.E.) who gave the name Carolingian (from the Latin "Caralos") to the Dynasty which ruled the Franks for the next two hundred years. Charles the Great (Charlemagne) continued his father's alliance with the pope. When fighting broke out between the pope and Lombards, Charles marched an

43

army into northern Italy and named himself king of the Franks and Lombards (774 C.E.). Having dispelled the Lombard threat he marched his army across the Pyrenees and pushed the Muslims out of northern Spain (795 C.E.). Charlemagne established the Spanish Mark, or March, as the frontier between Muslim and Christian Europe. Initially, Charlemagne was less successful in his campaigns east of the Rhine. After a long struggle (772 – 804 C.E.) his troops defeated the Saxons and won their conversion to Christianity. In 799 C.E. a mob of discontented Romans drove Pope Leo III out of the city. The pope appealed to Charlemagne. Charlemagne marched his army to Rome and punished the rebellious Roman nobles. On Christmas Day in 800 C.E. Pope Leo III placed a crown on Charles' head and named him Holy Roman Emperor (Augustus). Historians dispute whether Charlemagne or Leo III instigated this action. Twelve years later the Byzantine Emperor, Michael I, agreed in the Treaty of Aix-la-Chapelle to recognize Charlemagne's authority as Western Emperor. Charlemagne died in 814 C.E.

5.1.5 *The Carolingian Empire*

Charlemagne's objective was to reestablish the Roman Empire in the West. He placed authority for the different parts of the Empire in 200 counts (each count was in charge of a county). Royal messengers (*missi dominici*) periodically visited the counts. Charlemagne assembled his leading advisors around him at his court at Aix-la-Chapelle (Achen). He ordered that schools be established to insure that there would be a supply of educated administrators. Charlemagne's son, Louis the Pious, succeeded his father. Louis's reign (814 – 840 C.E.) was marred by disputes between his three sons for control of the Empire. Louis's death (840 C.E.) sparked a civil war over how his estate was to be divided. Louis's younger sons, Louis the German and Charles the Bald, sided against their brother Lothair. Charles and Louis defeated Lothair at the Battle of Fonteney in 841 C.E. In the Oath of Strasbourg (842), Louis the German

THE CAROLINGIAN EMPIRE

Frankish Kingdom circa 768
Areas conquered by Charlemagne
Tributary peoples
Byzantine Empire

and Charles the Bald renewed their alliance. The Oath of Strasbourg is the earliest European document written in Old French
and Old High German. In 842 C.E. the three brothers signed an
accord (the Treaty of Verdun) which created three kingdoms.
Charles was given control of the Western Kingdom (France).
Louis received the Eastern Kingdom (Germany). Charles and
Louis compensated Lothair with the Middle Kingdom (a narrow stretch of land that reached from the North Sea to the
Mediterranean).

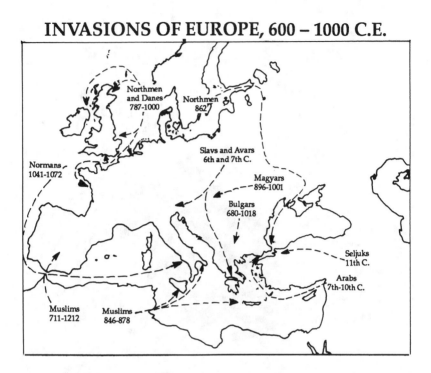

5.1.6 *Europe in the Ninth and Tenth Centuries*

Europe was threatened from three different directions during the ninth and tenth centuries. The Vikings attacked from the north. Muslim armies resumed their advance in the south and the Magyars struck from the east. Of the three, the Vikings had the greatest impact on Europe's development in these centuries. The Danes occupied what is now Denmark during the fifth and sixth centuries. By 600 C.E. they controlled most of Scandinavia. Viking raids on Western Europe began in earnest after 790 C.E. These attacks led Charlemagne to commission a coast guard. After 840 C.E. the Viking raids lost their sporadic character. Viking fleets carried large armies into combat. The Danish Vikings occupied England leaving only Wessex under the control of the English king, Alfred (871 – 899 C.E.). Norse Vikings captured the Shetland Islands, Ireland, and colonized Iceland. Swedish Vikings moved across the Baltic and established their hold over much of Poland. In 896 C.E. Danish

Vikings captured control of the mouth of the River Seine. They forced the Frankish king to grant them Normandy and Brittany. In the eleventh century, the Normans drove the Byzantine army out of southern Italy and Sicily, while another Norman army, under the leadership of William the Conqueror, conquered England (Battle of Hastings in 1066 C.E.) The Viking invasions left France divided into small principalities. The renewal of Muslim attacks in the south endangered Europe's security. The Magyars attacked the descendants of Louis the German. Otto the Great (936 – 973 C.E.) stopped the Magyar advance. Otto established the Saxons as the most powerful force in Western Europe. In 962 C.E. he assumed the title of Holy Roman Emperor.

5.2 ECONOMIC LIFE IN THE EARLY MIDDLE AGES

5.2.1 *Decline of Cities*

Rome's collapse ushered in a period in which cities declined in population and much of Europe returned to subsistence agriculture. After ca. 600 C.E., roads fell into disrepair and trade in goods (barter economy) replaced the Roman money economy. Towns lost their political and economic importance. The few cities that remained gained their significance because they were the residences of bishops or noblemen. The Carolingian rulers continued this tendency by establishing their courts in the countryside.

5.2.2 *Agriculture*

Agricultural productivity fell during the early Middle Ages. The decline in trade encouraged a shift from the Roman field-grazing system (based on animal husbandry) to subsistence agriculture.

5.2.3 *Manorialism and Feudalism*

Manorialism developed throughout Europe in the early Middle Ages. Manorialism refers to a system of economic organization. The large estates and public lands that had existed under the Roman Empire became the king's property. Kings awarded these estates to those who had performed a special service or to insure the loyalty of powerful nobles. The political system of personal relationships between lords and vassals was called feudalism. Nobles swore an oath of fealty to the king and received in return a fief (right to control an estate). Manorialism was an economic system in which estates strove for self-sufficiency. Feudalism describes the system of personal ties and obligations which bound vassals to their lords. Serfs were peasants who were bound to the land on which they worked. Serfs paid (usually a certain number of days of labor each week) a robot which gave them the right to work their own fields. The nobles were responsible for providing for the serfs in times of difficulty.

5.3 THE CHURCH

5.3.1 *The Rise of the Papacy*

During the early Middle Ages the power of the papacy increased. The Church was the single institution that survived the Germanic invasions intact. The pope played a central role in keeping the idea of a unified Empire alive in the West. In 375 C.E., Pope Damasus I claimed that the pope held the supreme teaching authority in Christendom. Damasus based his claim on the Petrine Doctrine, in which Christ described Peter as the "rock" on which the Church would be built. Gregory I (590-640 C.E.) was the first member of a monastical order to rise to the papacy. Gregory the Great's accomplishments earned him a position as one of the four Church Fathers (others include Jerome, Ambrose, and Augustine). Gregory advanced the idea of penance and the concept of purgatory. He centralized the Church's administration and was the first pope to rule as the secular head of Rome as well as of the lands surrounding the city. Gregory's careful statecraft helped him outmaneuver the Lombards who threatened to overrun his holdings. Gregory threw his support behind the Benedictine order. In a time when communications between the different parts of Europe were collapsing, Gregory used the Benedictines to create the institutional basis for a Western-oriented Latin Church. Under Gregory I England was Christianized (visit of the second St. Augustine in 596).

5.3.2 *Monasticism*

Monasticism originated in the Near East. The initial monks were motivated by a desire to live simple lives devoted to the worship of God. Benedict of Nursia (480 – 543 C.E.) established the basis of Western monasticism. In 529 C.E. he released his "Rule" which presented a guide for a monk's daily life. All monks vowed to follow the abbot's (leader of the chapter house) authority. In the eighth century, Charles Martel recognized that the Bendictines could help in his effort to subdue the pagan Saxons. He promised to supply financial support to St. Boniface in return for Boniface's help in reaching Martel's territorial objectives. Charles Martel did not live long enough to enjoy the benefits of this alliance. In 751 C.E. Boniface repaid his debt by placing a crown on the head of Charles Martel's son, Pepin. Forty nine years later, Pope Leo III named Charlemagne Holy Roman Emperor.

5.3.3 *Disputes with the Eastern Church*

Throughout the sixth and seventh centuries the pope acknowledged that the Byzantine Emperor was the leader of the Roman Empire. From Gregory I onwards the pope's secular power grew. Increasingly, the papacy recognized the importance of the Germanic tribes. Tension between the Eastern and Western Churches was apparent after the Council of Constantinople (680 – 681 C.E.). The Orthodox patriarch declared Pope Honarius guilty of heresy for having claimed that the pope possessed an infallible teaching authority. The other patriarchs (leaders of the Church in Alexandria, Ephesus, Antioch, and Constantinople) disputed the pope's claim to spiritual ascendancy. The Iconoclasm Controversy (726 – 843 C.E.) exasperated the relations between the two branches of Christendom. Pope Stephen II (752 – 757 C.E.) forged an alliance with the Frankish Kingdom. In 756 the Donation of Pepin granted the pope control over the the Vatican state. Stephen justified the pope's right to exercise secular power on the basis of the forged *Donation of Constantine*. In the *Donation of Constantine* it was alleged that the emperor had given the pope control of Rome and the western part of the Roman Empire. In 800 C.E. Pope Leo III declared the emperor's throne vacant and named Charlemagne emperor. The end of the Iconoclasm Controversy (843 C.E.) brought a short improvement in the relations between Rome and Constantinople. The publication of the pseudo-Isidoric decretals (forged papal canons, 847 – 852 C.E.) and the request in 864 C.E. by Boris, khan of the Bulgars, for an interpretation of the Nicene Creed precipitated a new crisis. Conditions continued to worsen until 1054 when the two churches underwent a final schism.

5.3.4 *Currents of Reform within the Latin Church*

Benedict of Aniane (816 – 817 C.E.) led the movement which called for reform of the monasteries. Benedict and his followers believed that the monasteries had become too involved in secular and temporal affairs. They called for strict compliance with the *Rule of St. Benedict*. A century later a second reform movement grew up around a newly founded monastery at Cluny (in France). The Cluniac movement established more than two hundred monasteries. The individual monasteries were governed by priors who were under the direction of a single abbot. Eventually more than 1500 monasteries were attached to Cluny.

5.4 CULTURE IN THE EARLY MIDDLE AGES

During the early Middle Ages, literacy nearly disappeared in Western Christendom. Factors such as the decline of cities, the breakdown in trade, and the subsistence economy in most of the West offer a partial explanation for the cultural decline. Monasteries were the repositories of the few elements of antiquity that survived the general decline. Outside of the monasteries the two most important literary works of this period were *Beowulf* (ca. 700 C.E.) and the Venerable Bede's (635 – 673 C.E.) *History of England*.

5.4.1 *The Carolingian Renaissance*

During the eighth and ninth centuries the Carolingian emperors inspired a revival in learning. Charlemagne summoned Alcuin, an English scholar, to organize the intellectual life at his court. Alcuin established a number of monastical schools which supplied the Carolingians with able administrators. During this period, Einhard (ca. 793 C.E.) wrote a biography of Charlemagne that provides a detailed portrait of the king's life and times. Manuscript illumination (painted illustrations) was the chief outlet for artistic energies in the early Middle Ages. The Irish *Book of Kells* (ca. 750 C.E.) is probably the greatest surviving example of this tradition. Science and technology came to a standstill during this period in the Latin West. Medicine in the West fell into superstition while Islamic physicians were making major advances. The Germanic tribes were typical of most of the Europeans in their belief that sickness was caused either by elves, worms, or the number 9.

5.5   EUROPE IN THE ELEVENTH CENTURY

By 1050 Europe was emerging from the five centuries of decline that followed Rome's collapse. Throughout this period, Rome's two heirs in the East (Byzantium and Islam) were vastly superior to the West. The brief Carolingian Empire was too short to have created the basis for a revitalized West. In 1050 the West was on the verge of overcoming its Eastern rivals. A new dynasty (the Capet) controlled France. The Normans were poised to launch overseas campaigns in the Mediterranean and against England. In Central Europe, the German Saxon kings had defeated the Hungarians and were consolidating their power in Germany. A new age was about to dawn.

CHRONOLOGY OF
THE EARLY MIDDLE AGES

410	Alaric and Visigoths loot Rome
455	Vandals sack Rome
476	Last Western Roman Emperor (Romulus Augustulus) deposed
493 – 525	Theodoric king of Ostrogoths (Italy)
481 – 511	Clovis first king of Franks (France)
ca. 500	Arthur king of England
ca. 500 – 700	Decline of towns
511 – 729	Frankish (Merovingian) Do-Nothing kings Rise to power of Mayors of the Palace
673 – 735	Venerable Bede
ca. 700	*Beowulf*
700 – 1050	Predominance of subsistence agriculture
714 – 744	Charles Martel "the Hammer"
732	Battle of Tours and Poitiers
750	Irish *Book of Kells*
751 – 768	Pepin the Short

751	Pope Zachary crowns Pepin King of the Franks
768 – 814	Charlemagne; Expansion of Frankish Empire
774	Charlemagne conquers the Lombards (northern Italy)
772 – 804	Saxon Wars
787	Beginning of Viking Raids
795	Spanish March
800	Pope Leo III crowns Charlemagne Holy Roman emperor
814 – 840	Louis the Pious
ca. 840	Struggle between Louis's sons for Empire
842	Oath of Strasbourg
843	Treaty of Verdun
841 – 896	Viking invasions
871 – 899	Alfred the Great in England
936 – 973	Otto I first Saxon king of Germanic Lands
987 – 996	Hugh Capet first Capetian king of France

CHAPTER 6

ECONOMY AND SOCIETY IN THE HIGH MIDDLE AGES

6.1   POPULATION GROWTH

The population of Europe grew rapidly during the high Middle Ages. At the end of the tenth century there were probably 38 million people living in Western Europe (including Kievian Russia). By the mid-fourteenth century the population had jumped to more than 75 million. A number of factors caused this population increase. Agricultural production increased as more efficient agricultural technologies became widespread and new lands were brought under cultivation.

6.2   THE MEDIEVAL AGRICULTURAL REVOLUTION

As in all civilizations prior to the nineteenth century, agriculture provided the basis of the medieval economy. A series of technological innovations (new sources of power, new machines, and a new system of cultivation) produced the economic prosperity of the high Middle Ages. Many of these innovations were devised early in the medieval period. It was not, however, until after 1050 that they became sufficiently widespread to produce a qualitative effect.

6.2.1 *New Sources of Power*

Early in the eleventh century Europeans began to exploit the potential of water and wind power. The Romans used water as a source of power in mills. Most of the Roman water wheels fell into disuse during the early Middle Ages. After 1050 northern Europeans began to put water to a number of different uses. By the thirteenth century, water mills were operating in the textile industry for fulling (beating a cloth in water to prevent shrinkage). In the fourteenth century, water was employed to drive sawmills and the bellows used to smelt iron. Windmills were developed during this period. The Islamic scholar Al Musadi (d. 957 C.E.) wrote an encyclopedic work in which he described windmills. Windmills did not find their way to the West for two centuries. The earliest European windmills appeared in Normandy around 1180 C.E.

6.2.2 *New Machines*

Throughout antiquity peasants used the "scratch plow" in their cultivation of the land. "Scratch plows" were well suited to the sandy, porous soil of the Mediterranean lands. Northern Europe possessed a much heavier, denser soil which required a heavy plow. Heavy plows were employed during the early Middle Ages. Their use was dramatically extended in the ninth and tenth centuries. Climatic change partially accounts for the introduction of heavy plows. Climatologists believe that Europe experienced a warming trend between 700 and 1200 C.E. The average temperature probably rose one degree centigrade. This small change in temperature meant that there were more sunny days, less rainfall, and a longer growing season. These factors combined to make the Northern European plain an attractive area for expansion. The heavy plow had additional advantages. Fields cultivated with a scratch plow must be plowed in two different directions. The heavy plow was able to prepare the field in one plowing.

6.2.3 The Use of Horses in Agriculture

The introduction of horses into agricultural labor occurred during this period. In antiquity horses were harnessed in the same way as cattle and oxen. The horse's higher neck placed a physical limit on how great a load a horse could pull before strangling itself. Sometime after 800 C.E. padded collars were introduced. The padded collar meant that horses could be used in conjunction with the heavy plow. One of the advantages that horses have over oxen as team animals is that they move at a faster gait. Horses possess the disadvantage that they require a more nutritious diet and are more susceptible to hoof disease than oxen in the wet, muddy European environment. This meant that it was necessary to introduce new crops (oats) and shoe the horses. Both of these disadvantages proved to be challenges which the peasant farmers were able to overcome.

6.2.4 The Three Field System

In antiquity, Greek and Roman farmers employed a two field system. One field was cultivated while the other lay fallow. During the high Middle Ages the three field system became common. The three field system has several advantages. First, only one-third of the total acreage lies fallow. Second, farmers reduced the risk of crop failure. In the three field system one crop (a grain or cereal) was planted in the fall while a second crop (legumes or oats) was planted in the spring. Finally, the three field system had the additional advantage of reducing unproductive labor. A field that is left fallow must be plowed twice each year in order to keep the weeds down and prepare the soil for the next season. Under the three field system farmers could devote less of their time to plowing unproductive acreage.

6.2.5 *Agricultural Productivity*

These technological innovations greatly increased agricultural productivity. The rapid increase in population attests to this. Population grows when fertility rates increase and/or mortality rates decline. Historians have found evidence that supports the conclusion that the overall life expectancy of Europeans declined in the high Middle Ages compared to the early Middle Ages. Only 9.3% of males and 10.5% of females survived their sixtieth birthday in the period of 1000 to 1345 C.E. as opposed to 16.9% of males and 16.4% of females between 751 to 1000 C.E. The great difference between the early and high Middle Ages lay in the increase in the number of babies that lived past their first year. Some demographers estimate that 40% of the population in 1200 C.E. was under fourteen years of age (as compared with less than 20% in 1998). These figures reinforce the conclusion that the technological innovations had increased productivity. Proportionally fewer peasant farmers were producing a substantially larger agricultural surplus. This surplus had the added benefit of freeing peasants from their agricultural pursuits and opening new possibilities of work in manors and in villages and towns.

6.3   CHANGES IN MANORIALISM IN THE HIGH MIDDLE AGES

The manor and the village were the two most important forms of economic organization in the high Middle Ages. A manor refers to the holdings of a single noble. Manors varied in size. Some were so small that they included only a single village. Large manors might incorporate several villages. Manorialism was an economic system and should not be considered a synonym for feudalism (decentralized system of political authority). The conditions in manors varied. The lands surrounding the village and nobleman's manor house were usually divided into long strips. A portion of the land was left as common pasture and woodland. The land's ownership was divided between the manor's lord and the serfs (sometimes called villeins). The lord's property was called his demesne. The demesne consisted of one-third to one-half of the total estate. Serfs were required to work three or four days a week on the lord's demesne. In return they received the right to cultivate their own fields.

6.3.1 *The Peasants*

Most Europeans during the high Middle Ages followed agricultural pursuits. Manors were self-sufficient. Besides producing their food requirements, peasant craftsmen manufactured whatever other products were needed. Peasant labor was generally communal. The open field system (where the narrow strips were separated only by narrow untilled areas) reinforced this tendency. Serfs shared machinery and worked on one another's land. A portion of the manor was designated as "commons." Peasants could graze their animals on this land. Serfs showed their submission to the manor's lord in a variety of ways. Besides working on the lord's demesne, serfs paid dues and taxes to their lord and were under the lord's legal jurisdiction. Serfs lived in dilapidated dwellings. Bread and porridge were the staples of their diet. These conditions gradually improved during the high Middle Ages. The growing agricultural surplus meant that the serfs' food supply became both more secure and varied. The bringing of new lands into cultivation presented many peasants with new opportunities. In Germany and northern France nobles had to find inducements which would cause serfs to move to previously uncultivated regions. The practice of enfranchisement (freeing) of serfs grew during this period. The new lands offered the opportunity for other serfs to simply run away from their lord's manor. These serfs could find employment as agricultural workers on new estates. In some areas, such as England, the process of freeing serfs from their medieval obligations moved rapidly. In other places the serfs' obligations continued until the 18th and 19th centuries (Russia).

6.3.2 *The Clergy*

The condition of the clergy varied in the high Middle Ages. Every village had its church. The priests who led these congregations were not much more sophisticated than their fellow communicants. The great ecclesiastical princes who governed the cathedrals and abbeys were as powerful as any of the medieval nobles. During the high Middle Ages the papacy increased its secular role. The Cistercians (after 1098) and the Carthusians (1094 C.E.) continued to keep the monastic reform movement alive. Early in the thirteenth century, Francis of Assisi organized the Franciscans, or Minorite mendicant order. Francis's ideal was to pattern his life after Jesus. Unlike the aristocratic monastical orders which established their monasteries in the countryside, the Franciscans worked among the poor and homeless in cities. In 1223 C.E., Pope Honorius III granted Francis's request to form an order. Seven years earlier the pope had established the Dominican Order. The pope created the Dominican Order to lead the fight against heresy (the Albigensians in southern France between 1209 and 1229 C.E.).

6.3.3 *The Aristocracy*

The growing prosperity of the eleventh and twelfth centuries helped transform the aristocracy. The nobility was divided into the High Nobility (great hereditary Germanic lords) and the Lower Nobility that developed from among those who had performed services to the large territorial nobles. During the eleventh century, knights developed as a class of professional warriors. In the twelfth century the nobility's appetite for internal warfare slackened. Pope Urban II called on the nobility to fight against the Muslims. The idea of chivalry developed as one of the alternatives to the old fighting tradition. The word chivalry, originally used to convey the ideal conduct associated with the medieval class of knights, later came to embrace any type of honorable, virtuous, or courteous behavior. The Code of Chivalry called for the Christian knight to be proficient as a horseman and warrior as well as kind, virtuous, and gentle.

6.3.4 *Women*

The Code of Chivalry marked an important change in the attitude towards women. Most women in the high Middle Ages lived lives of unremitting drudgery and toil. During the eleventh century, upper-class women became objects of veneration in the courtly tradition. Some women, such as Eleanor of Aquitaine, played an active political role. Eleanor governed England from 1190 to 1194 C.E., while her son, Richard the Lionhearted, fought in the Crusades.

6.4 CITIES AND TOWNS

The extensive system of roads that the Romans constructed collapsed during the early Middle Ages. One of the clearest signs of the revival of trade and the importance of cities in the eleventh and twelfth centuries was the renewed interest in road building and construction. The Romans built roads in order to provide a communications link to the different parts of their empire. In the high Middle Ages roads were designed as a system of transport. Cities grew rapidly. South of the Alps, in the period from 1050 to 1300 C.E., city states such as Genoa, Pisa, and Venice opened trading relationships with the Far East.

The Crusades stimulated an appetite for luxury goods. Roads meant easier access to markets. Trade fairs helped transform provincial villages into towns. Between 1100 and 1200 C.E. Paris, London, and Cologne doubled their population. Italian cities grew at a faster pace, with Venice, Genoa, and Milan having populations greater than 100,000. Guilds controlled the economic life in medieval cities. Guilds were divided into craft (a single profession such as wheelwrights) and trade (groups of merchants). The medieval guild and chamber of commerce established the "just" price for goods and services as part of its responsibility to regulate the city's trade. The guild system provided a mechanism for the recruitment of apprentices, their training, and, finally, the production of a "masterpiece" which demonstrated that the individual was a "master" of his craft.

6.4.1 *The Return to a Money Economy*

In the early Middle Ages the economy reverted to a barter system. By the twelfth century gold coins were in circulation in Italy. The use of hard currency was another sign of Europe's economic revival.

CHRONOLOGY OF THE CHURCH IN THE EARLY MIDDLE AGES

325	Four patriarchs (Jerusalem, Antioch, Alexandria, Rome) given "spiritual equality" by Council of Nicaea
ca. 375	Pope Damasus asserts he is supreme teaching authority
	Beginning of the evolution of papacy
440 – 461	Leo I claims pope's primacy
389 – 461	St. Patrick brings Christianity to Ireland
480 – 543	St. Benedict establishes basis of Western monasticism

590 – 640	Gregory I becomes the first monastical pope
597	Gregory sends St. Augustine to England (Canterbury)
	Gregory centralizes Church's administration, becoming secular ruler of Rome
680 – 681	6th Ecumenical Council of Constantinople condemns the Eastern Emperor Heraclius
	Orthodox patriarch responds by condemning pope as heretic
	Contests pope's claim to be an infallible teaching authority
752 – 757	Pope Stephen II turns from East
756	Donation of Pepin (Papal States)
800	Leo III crowns Charlemagne Holy Roman Emperor
816 – 817	Benedict of Anaine calls for reform
847 – 852	Pseudo – Isidoric decretals: forged evidence supporting pope's claim to primacy
900 – 1100	Cluniac Movement
1046	Beginning of period of Reform Papacy
1084	Formation of the Carthusians
1098	Formation of the Cistercians
1096 – 1291	Period of the Crusades

CHAPTER 7

THE HIGH MIDDLE AGES: POLITICAL DEVELOPMENTS

7.1 MAIN TENDENCIES OF THE HIGH MIDDLE AGES

At the beginning of the eleventh century, Europe was inferior in most respects to the Byzantine Empire and the Islamic civilization. By 1300 C.E. the Europeans had surpassed both. During the high Middle Ages (ca. 1050 – 1300) Europe experienced phenomenal economic, political and social progress.

7.2 THE HOLY ROMAN EMPIRE

The Treaty of Verdun (843 C.E.) insured that Charlemagne's grandson, Louis the German, would serve as Holy Roman Emperor. Louis's descendants were weak leaders and were unable to prevent the dukes of the five great German duchies (Saxony, Franconia, Swabia, Bavaria, and the Loraine) from eroding the emperor's power. In 911 C.E. the last Carolingian died.

7.2.1 *The Saxon Dynasty*

The German dukes elected (911 C.E.) the weakest of their number (Conrad of Franconia) to lead the German lands. In 919 C.E. Henry the Fowler (duke of Saxony) succeeded Conrad. Henry was the first in a line of Saxon emperors which ran from 919 to 1024 C.E. Henry led successful campaigns against the Vikings, Slavs, and Magyars. Henry's son, Otto, continued his father's policies when he became king in 936 C.E. In 939 C.E. Otto suppressed a revolt by the other dukes and sixteen years later he won a decisive victory over the Magyars (955 C.E.). A revolt in Rome gave Otto the pretext he needed to open an Italian campaign. In 962 C.E. he was crowned Holy Roman Emperor. Otto's descendants governed the Empire until 1024 C.E., when the duke of Franconia, Conrad II (1024 – 1039 C.E.) was chosen to lead the Empire.

7.2.2 *The Franconian Dynasty*

The Franconian Dynasty reigned from 1024 until 1125 C.E. Henry III (1039 – 1056 C.E.) and Henry IV (1056 – 1106 C.E.) were the most notable of the Franconian rulers. Henry III was a capable administrator and continued his father's policy of aiding the pope. Henry III called on ecclesiastical authorities to correct the abuses present within the church. When Henry III died his son, Henry IV, was only six years old. The regency of Henry IV gave the German dukes an opportunity to plunder the king's holdings. When Henry IV reached his majority he faced two problems: First, he needed to reverse the setbacks he had received at the hands of the dukes. Second, he had to overcome the Pope's assault on his imperial authority.

7.2.3 *The Investiture Controversy*

The pope and emperor were most divided over the issue of lay investiture (where monarchs chose high church officials

THE GERMAN EMPIRE, circa 1200 C.E.

within their realm). Pope Gregory VII was determined to strip secular leaders of this power. Gregory's predecessor Leo X had proclaimed the absolute "primacy" of St. Peter. In 1073 C.E. Gregory announced his intention to enforce the ban on lay investiture. The ban applied to all Christian rulers. Gregory elected to apply it only to Henry IV. When Henry refused to accede to his demands Gregory excommunicated the emperor and encouraged Henry's subjects to rebel. In 1077 C.E. Gregory compelled Henry to cross the Alps and come to Canossa. Henry waited for three days in the snow before Gregory agreed to hear Henry's appeal for forgiveness. The investiture controversy illustrated how much the pope's power had grown from the early Middle Age. In 1083 C.E. Henry brought an army into Italy and had his revenge. He captured Rome and sent Gregory into exile. Gregory took refuge with the Normans in southern Italy where he died two years later. Henry IV, however, failed in his efforts to restore the emperor's prerogatives. The Concordat of Worms (1122 C.E.) resolved the dispute over lay investiture. The Concordat gave the pope control of the bishops in northern Italy while the emperor retained the right to invest bishops in Germany with their scepters (symbol of earthly authority) but not with their rings and staffs (the symbols of religious authority).

7.2.4 *The Hohenstaufen Emperors*

In 1125 C.E. the last Franconian emperor died. Two families competed for the vacant throne: the Welfs and Hohenstaufens. The election of the Hohenstaufen candidate, Conrad III (1138 – 1152 C.E.) started a brief civil war between the two factions' supporters. Conrad III prevailed. Frederick I (called Barbarossa because of his red beard) was his successor. Barbarossa was chosen emperor because his mother was a Welf and his father a Hohenstaufen. He brought the revolt to an end, stopped the Viking advances, and marched across the Alps and secured northern Italy. The pope allied himself with Frederick's enemies in northern Italy. The pope joined the Lombard League because he feared the expansion of Barbarossa's power. In 1176 C.E. the Lombard league defeated Frederick's supporters. Barbarossa retained control of southern Italy and Sicily. Frederick II (1210 – 1250 C.E.) was the last important Hohenstaufen leader. In 1220 C.E. he was crowned Holy Roman Emperor. In 1226 C.E. the pope directed him to lead a crusade. The pope excommunicated Frederick because Frederick had returned from the Holy Land without winning any military victories. Frederick II, however, was able to gain in negotiations what the Crusader armies could not achieve on the battlefield. Frederick II persuaded the Islamic leaders to grant Jerusalem to the Christians. This settlement did not win the pope's approval and Frederick II was once again excommunicated. When he died, in 1239 C.E., he was still at war with the pope. The Hohenstaufen Dynasty survived for another eighteen years. Charles of Anjou (brother of Louis IX of France) and the pope defeated the last Hohenstaufen (Conradin). He was executed in Naples. In 1273 C.E. Rudolf von Hapsburg became emperor. The Hapsburg Dynasty controlled the Holy Roman Empire until 1806 C.E.

7.3   ENGLAND

7.3.1   *England Prior to 1066*

The Romans abandoned their last outpost in England late in the fourth century. The Jutes, Angles, and Saxons occupied different parts of England around 450 C.E. (the time of the legendary King Arthur). The Vikings began to make periodic raids in 793 C.E. Communication with the continent improved under King Egbert of Wessex. Egbert had lived in Charlemagne's court. Egbert won control of the Angles and Saxons. His successor, Alfred the Great (871 – 899 C.E.), defeated the Danes in 878 C.E. In 959 C.E. Edgar the Great became the first king of all England. The Danish threat reappeared early in the eleventh century. After defeating Ethelrod the Unready in 1013 C.E., the Danes forced the English to pay heavy taxes (Danegeld). Edward the Confessor ruled England between 1042 and 1066 C.E. Powerful earls who controlled vast estates restricted Edward's power. When Edward died William, duke of Normandy, and Harold of England both claimed to be his rightful heir. William brought an army to England to enforce his claim. On October 14, 1066 Harold was killed in the Battle of Hastings and William became king of England.

7.3.2 Norman England

William's victory opened a new phase in English history. The old Anglo-Saxon nobility was stripped of its privileges. William instituted feudalism. He ordered his vassals to pledge their fealty to him in the Oath of Salisbury (1086 C.E.). In return, the vassals received a fief (an estate) and accepted the obligation to come to their liege lord's aid. William ordered an inventory of all the property in the kingdom which was recorded in the *Domesday Book* (1086 C.E.). William's descendants, William II (1087 – 1100C.E.) and Henry I (1100 – 1135 C.E.), continued their father's program of centralization. Notable in this process was Henry I's creation of the Office of Exchequer to monitor the receipt of taxes from the local officials (sheriffs).

7.3.3 The Plantagenets

Nineteen years of civil war followed Henry's death in 1135 C.E. In 1154 C.E. Henry I's grandson, Henry II, was crowned king. Henry was the first king in the Plantagenet Dynasty. From his father's family he inherited England. Henry acquired Normandy and Brittany from his mother. Henry II's rule was marked with controversy. Henry II struggled with the pope for control of the English clergy. Henry's childhood friend, Thomas Becket, became his adversary when the pope named Becket Archbishop of Canterbury. In 1170 C.E. four of Henry's knights murdered Becket. The public outcry was immediate and Henry faced opposition on every side. In 1173 – 1174 C.E. Henry's sons organized a revolt against their father. Henry suppressed the revolt. In 1189 C.E. Richard the Lionhearted succeeded his father. Richard was occupied fighting in the Holy Land during most of his reign. It is a tribute to Henry that the government continued to function smoothly during Richard's absence. John I (1199 – 1216 C.E.) became king after his brother's death. On June 15, 1215 the English barons compelled John to acknowledge their "ancient" privileges in the Magna Carta Libertatum. The Magna Carta established the principle that the English monarch's powers are limited. In 1216 Henry II became King. During Henry's fifty-six year reign (1216 – 1272 C.E.) the Church increased its power. Henry's efforts to gain the German crown provoked a rebellion among the English barons between 1258 and 1265 C.E. In 1272 Edward I became King. Edward I created the basis for a strong national monarchy. His need for new sources of revenue and his sense of popular opinion led him to convene a Parliament of English nobles. The Parliament served as a check on abuses of royal power while supplying Edward with the money he needed to run the government.

7.4 FRANCE

7.4.1 *The Capetian Dynasty*

The process of creating a strong national monarchy moved at a slower pace in France than in England in the high Middle Ages. In 987 C.E. Hugh Capet established the Capetian Dynasty (from the Latin "cappa" for cape). The early Capetian kings had little power until after 1108 C.E., when Louis the Fat (1108 – 1137 C.E.) subdued his most powerful vassals. With Abbot Suger of St. Denis as his chief advisor, Louis began the process of creating a national consciousness. Louis's grandson, Philip Augustus (1180 – 1223 C.E.) defeated King John of England (Battle of Bouvines) and won a large amount of territory in western France. The new territories were allowed to remain autonomous. Philip governed these lands through government officials called baillis. Between 1201 and 1229 C.E. the king led the crusade against the Albigensians in southern France. The Albigensians were a Christian sect that the pope judged heretical because of their denial of the existence of purgatory and their efforts to organize their lives according to the Sermon on the Mount. The murder of a papal legal advisor precipitated the Albigensian Crusade. In 1229 the Albigensians were destroyed. Philip Augustus was succeeded by his son, Louis VIII (1223 C.E.). Louis VIII conquered most of southern France during his three year reign. His successor, Louis IX (called Saint Louis because of his piety) reigned between 1226 and 1270 C.E. Under his leadership France enjoyed a period of economic prosperity and internal peace. Unfortunately, Philip IV (1285 – 1314 C.E.) lacked his grandfather's ability to govern. Philip IV's effort to expand France's influence led to a series of wars. Like his contemporary Edward I, Philip IV called for a national assembly (the Estates General). This body did not develop into an institution that offered a counter to the king's authority. In 1328 C.E. the Capetian dynasty ended with the death of Charles IV. The question of who was the rightful heir led to the outbreak of the Hundred Years' War between England and France.

7.5   SPAIN

Successive waves of Germanic invaders occupied Spain in the fourth, fifth, and sixth centuries. After 589 C.E. the Visigoths controlled the Iberian peninsula. In 710 C.E. the Muslim leader, Tarik, led his army across the Straits of Gibraltar (eight miles separate Africa and Spain at this point) and conquered Spain and Portugal.

7.5.1   *Muslim Spain*

Under the Muslims (Moors) Spain enjoyed both prosperity and good government. Abd-ar-Rahman (only surviving member of the Omayyad caliph's family) founded the Caliphate of Cordoba in 756 C.E. Between 756 and 1031 C.E. Cordoba became a center of scientific and intellectual activity. Cordoba had a population of more than 500,000 people while London and Paris had populations of no more than 15,000. Baghdad and

THE RECONQUEST OF SPAIN

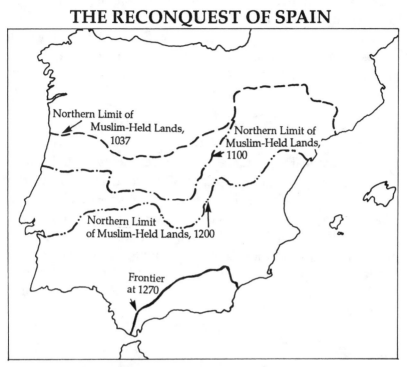

Cairo were Cordoba's only rivals. Internal dissent led to the collapse of the Caliphate of Cordoba in 1031 C.E. Spain was divided into more than twenty Muslim states.

7.5.2 *The Reconquista or Christian Reconquest of Spain*

Sancho the Great of Castile (1000 – 1035 C.E.) used the collapse of the caliphate of Cordoba as an opportunity to expand his territory. In 1063 C.E. the pope issued a call for a crusade to liberate Spain from the Muslims. Rodrigo Diaz de Vivar, known as el Cid (ca. 1085), was the most famous of the Christian knights who waged war on the Muslims. Throughout the Reconquista (1085-1340 C.E.), the opposition to the Muslims was organized around four small Christian states: Navarre in the north; Aragon in the northeast; Castile in the center; and Portugal in the west. Each of these kingdoms had a cortes (an assembly of nobles, clergy and townspeople). In 1212 C.E. three of these states (Castile, Navarre, and Aragon) won a decisive victory over the Muslims in the Battle of Las Navas de Tolosa. The fall of Cordoba (1236 C.E.) completed the Reconquista with the exception of the small Muslim state of Granada.

7.6 EASTERN EUROPE AND RUSSIA

The political development of Eastern Europe and Russia during the high Middle Ages was different than the rest of Europe. Most of this region was never under Rome's control. The Germanic invasions cut off Eastern Europe and Russia from the West's influence. Eastern Orthodox missionaries carried Christianity to the Slavs. In the ninth century, Otto I encouraged the settlement of Germans in the East. The Teutonic Knights occupied Prussia and much of Poland during the thirteenth century.

7.6.1 *Poland*

In 966 Poland became a Christian state with the conversion of Miezko I (960 – 992 C.E.). Miezko I placed Poland under the pope's protection and made his kingdom "a friend of the Holy Roman Empire." This arrangement carried no feudal obligations. Relations between Poland and the Holy Roman Empire worsened after 1003 C.E. In 1025 C.E. Mieszko II (1025 – 1034 C.E.) was compelled to acknowledge his dependence on the Holy Roman Empire. During the Investiture Controversy, Poland sided with Gregory VII against the Emperor Henry IV. In the twelfth and thirteenth centuries power was divided between a number of powerful nobles. After 1226 C.E. the Teutonic Knights (1222 – 1410 C.E.) controlled most of Poland.

7.6.2 *Russia*

Vladimir (984 – 1015 C.E.) converted to Orthodox Christianity in 988 C.E. He established the basis of Kievian Russia. His successor expanded westwards in the eleventh century. Yaroslav the Wise (1019 – 1054 C.E.) made war on the Poles. After 1054 C.E. Russia broke into competing principalities. In 1221 C.E. the Mongols (Tartars) invaded Russia. The Mongols completed their conquest in 1245 C.E. This ended Russia's contacts with West until the rise of the Grand Duchy of Moscow almost a century later.

CHRONOLOGY OF POLITICAL DEVELOPMENTS IN THE HIGH MIDDLE AGES

Holy Roman Empire
(Germany and Italy)

919 – 1024	Saxon Dynasty
936 – 976	Otto the Great
1024 – 1125	Franconian Dynasty
1024 – 1039	Conrad II
1039 – 1056	Henry III
1056 – 1106	Henry IV
1125 – 1268	Hohenstaufen Dynasty
1137 – 1152	Conrad III
1152 – 1190	Frederick Barbarossa
1190 – 1197	Henry VI
1212 – 1250	Frederick II
1250 – 1254	Conrad IV
1268	Conradin executed by Charles of Anjou

England

1066 – 1087	William the Conquerer

1086	Oath of Salisbury
	Domesday Book
1087 – 1100	William II
1100 – 1137	Henry I
1154 – 1399	Plantagenet Dynasty
1154 – 1189	Henry II
1189 – 1199	Richard the Lionhearted
1199 – 1216	John
1216 – 1272	Henry III
1258 – 1265	Barons' uprising
1272 – 1307	Edward I
1307 – 1327	Edward II
1327 – 1377	Edward III
1377 – 1399	Richard II
1337 – 1453	Hundred Years' War

France

987 – 1328	Capetian Dynasty
987 – 996	Hugh Capet
996 – 1031	Robert II
1031 – 1060	Henry I
1060 – 1108	Philip I
1108 – 1137	Louis VI (the Fat)
1137 – 1180	Louis VII
1180 – 1223	Philip II (Augustus)
1209 – 1229	Albigensian Crusade
1223 – 1226	Louis VIII
1226 – 1270	Louis IX (St. Louis)
1285 – 1314	Philip IV (the Fair)
1314 – 1316	Louis X
1316	John
1317 – 1322	Philip V
1322 – 1328	Charles IV

Spain

756 – 1031	Emirate of Cordoba
1008 – 1028	Civil war among Arabs
1000 – 1035	Sancho the Great
1063 – 1492	Reconquista
	Pope calls for a Crusade to free Spain
1085	Rodrigo Diaz de Vivar (el Cid)
	Conquest of Toledo
1139	Alfonso king of Portugal
1212	Castile, Aragon, and Navarre unite
1236	Cordoba falls
1238	Seville falls
1492	Granada falls

Eastern Europe

950	Piast Dynasty
960 – 992	Miezko I
966	Poland becomes Christian
992 – 1025	Boleslav I
1013 – 1018	Conflict with Holy Roman Empire
1024	Poles occupy Kiev
1025 – 1034	Miesako II accepts dependence on Holy Roman Emperor
1034 – 1058	Casimir I
	Bohemians attack Poland
1058 – 1079	Boleslav II sides with pope against Henry IV
1079 – 1102	Vladislav Hermann
1102 – 1106	Zbigniev
1106 – 1138	Boleslav III
1138	Seniorate as supreme authority

Kievian Russia

984 – 1015	Vladimir
988	Vladimir is baptized
1011 – 1054	Yaroslav the Wise
	War with Poles
1054	Russia breaks into principalities
1226 – 1410	Teutonic Knights
1245	Mongol Invaders conquer Russia (Tartars)

CHAPTER 8

THE CHURCH IN THE HIGH MIDDLE AGES

8.1 THE CHURCH AS AN INSTITUTION

8.1.1 *The Rise of the Papacy*

At the beginning of the eleventh century the Church was the largest landowner in Europe. The Church's spiritual and secular authority influenced every facet of life. Early in the tenth century the Church's involvement in temporal affairs was scrutinized. The leaders of the Cluniac movement wanted to renew the Church's spiritual values. Ending simony (accepting bribes in order to receive Church offices) and the establishment of celibacy for the clergy were the two most important of the reformers' objectives. During this period the power of the papacy grew. Leo X (1049 – 1059 C.E.) brought on the schism with the Orthodox Church (1054 C.E.) when he asserted that the pope was supreme over the other patriarchs. Between 1073 and 1085 C.E., Gregory VII fought to end lay investiture. One of the major problems facing the papacy during the eleventh century was the continuous state of warfare among the various Christian principalities. In 1040 C.E. the pope proclaimed a Pax Dei (Peace of God) which placed women, children, travelers and priests under papal protection. The Pax Dei banned fighting between Wednesday night and Monday morning and on Holy Days (this left only ninety days a year for warfare). The Pax Dei, however, did not stop the warfare between Christians. Urban II devised a more ingenious alternative when he called on the Christian princes to free the Holy Land.

8.1.2 *New Religious Currents in the Church*

By 1100 C.E. the initial fervor of the Cluniac movement had ebbed. Two new monastical orders, the Carthusians (ca. 1084 C.E.) and the Cistercians (ca. 1100 C.E.), took up the cause of reform. The Carthusian brothers committed themselves to lives given to the care of the soul. St. Bernard of Clairvaux founded the Cistercians. By 1153 C.E. there were more than 343 Cistercian chapter houses. Both the Cistercians and the Carthusians were dedicated to living simple, austere existences.

8.1.3 *Christian Beliefs*

In the high Middle Ages the cult of the Virgin Mary eclipsed the veneration of individual saints. Mary was given a mediator's role between a sinful humanity and Jesus. The Cistercians made Mary their patron saint. Many cathedrals during this period were dedicated to "Notre Dame" (our Lady). The doctrine of transubstantiation (the belief that the bread and wine of the communion service are transformed into the Christ's flesh and blood after consecration) was advanced in the twelfth century.

8.2 THE CRUSADES

In 1074 Gregory the VII issued a call for the liberation of Jerusalem and the Church of the Holy Sepulcher. Gregory's struggle with Henry IV forced him to delay taking action. In 1095 C.E. the eastern emperor, Alexius Comnenus, requested aid from Pope Urban II to help him in his campaign against the Seljuk Turks. On November 26, 1095, Urban II addressed the Synod of Clermont. In a sermon entitled Deus lo Vol (God Wills it) Urban appealed to Christians to join the First Crusade (the Latin word "crux," which means cross, is the root for crusade). Between 1096 and 1300 there were seven major Crusades.

8.2.1 *The First Crusade*

Urban II's call for Christians to liberate the Holy Land generated an immense response. Many answered the pope's summons because they wanted to make a pilgrimage to Jerusalem. The pope's promise of a plenary indulgence (a promise that those who took part in the Crusade would be exempted from punishment in purgatory) attracted others. Estimates vary widely, but, according to Gen. W.A. Mitchell, writing in *World's Military History*, perhaps as many as 100,000 strong-armored horsemen enlisted in the First Crusade, in 1097.

Peter the Hermit. Peter the Hermit (a monk from Amiens in France) was unwilling to wait for the Crusader army's organization. He preached a series of fiery sermons which persuaded 30,000 peasants to follow him as he marched off to the Holy Land. The peasant crusaders robbed and massacred Jews as they passed through Germany. In Bulgaria they fell on local Christians, looting their homes and stealing their grain supplies. When they arrived in Constantinople, Alexius Comnenus ordered that they be immediately transported across the Bosphorus where the Seljuk Turks easily defeated them. The remnants of Peter's army were sold into slavery.

The Consequences of the First Crusade. The organized Crusader army reached Constantinople several months later. The Crusaders met fierce resistance. Jerusalem fell on July 15, 1099, after a five-week siege. The First Crusade was a success. The Europeans vanquished their foes. Many of the Crusaders were the younger sons of nobles. The practice of primogeniture (oldest inherits the father's entire estate) left many of the crusaders as hungry for an opportunity to make their fortune as they were to save their souls. The Crusaders established four Crusader states based on the French feudal model: the County of Edessa, the Principality of Antioch, the County of Tripoli, and the Latin Kingdom of Jerusalem.

8.2.2 Religious and Military Orders

The success of the First Crusade sparked a movement of pilgrims to the Holy Land. A number of religious, military orders were organized to aid and comfort the pilgrims. In 1113 C.E. Pope Pascal II granted the Knights of St. John (Hospitalers) the right to maintain a hospital in Jerusalem. The Hospitalers chose as their standard a white cross on a black background. The Knights of the Temple (ca. 1118) were called Templars because their chapter house was erected on the site of the Temple of Solomon. The Templars vowed to live in poverty and chastity. The sign for the Templars was a red cross on a white background. A group of German noblemen organized the Order of St. Mary of the Teutons (Teutonic Knights) in 1190. By the thirteenth century, the Teutonic Knights (distinguished from the other orders by a black cross on a white background) had shifted the center of their activity from the Holy Land to Eastern Europe.

8.2.3 The Second Crusade

The fall of Edessa (1144 C.E.) led to the Second Crusade (1147 – 1149 C.E.). Led by the German Emperor, Conrad II, the Crusaders failed to overcome their internal rivalries. The Crusade ended without recapturing Edessa.

8.2.4 *Saladin and the Third Crusade*

In 1185 C.E. the Muslim leader Saladin called on his people to drive the infidels (Christians) out of the Holy Land. In 1187 C.E. Saladin's army captured Jerusalem. This led Pope Innocent III to issue a call for the Third Crusade (1189 – 1192 C.E.). Philip Augustus (king of France), Frederick Barbarossa (the German emperor), and Richard the Lionhearted answered his summons. The Crusaders were unable to resolve their disagreements and Jerusalem remained under Muslim control. Richard the Lionhearted succeeded in negotiating the right of Christian pilgrims to visit their shrines in Jerusalem.

8.2.5 *The Fourth Crusade*

Pope Innocent III was unwilling to allow Jerusalem to remain in Muslim hands. In 1202 C.E. the pope renewed his call for a Crusade. The Crusaders (1202 – 1204 C.E.) never reached the Holy Land. The army assembled in Venice where the doge (leader of the maritime state) demanded payment for the soldiers' transportation to the Near East. The Crusaders lacked the money necessary for their passage. The Venetian merchants proposed that the Crusaders loot Constantinople and use the booty that they would gain to pay for their transportation. In one swift blow, the Venetian merchants hoped to rid themselves of their competition in the East and seize control of the Byzantine Empire's trading assets in the Mediterranean. In 1204 C.E. Constantinople fell. The Crusaders established the Latin kingdom of Constantinople. Fifty-seven years later the Byzantine Emperor's troops recaptured the city.

8.2.6 *The Later Crusades*

The crusading spirit did not disappear in 1204 C.E. In the

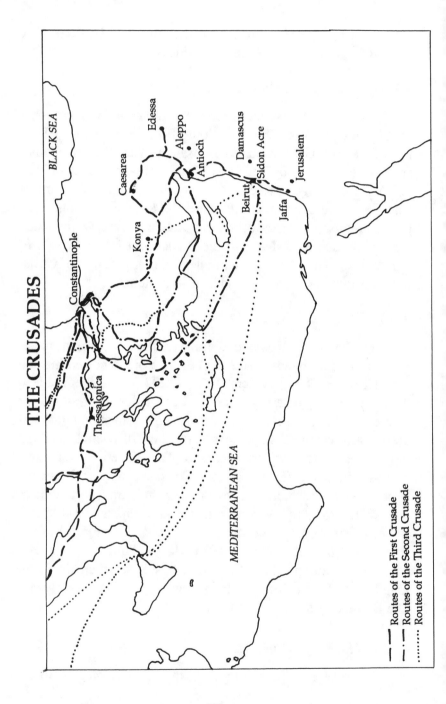

THE CRUSADES

BLACK SEA

Edessa

Aleppo

Antioch

Caesarea

Damascus

Sidon
Acre

Beirut

Jerusalem

Jaffa

Konya

Constantinople

Thessalonica

MEDITERRANEAN SEA

- - - Routes of the First Crusade
- · - Routes of the Second Crusade
· · · · · Routes of the Third Crusade

Fifth Crusade (1228 – 1229 C.E.) Frederick II succeeded in negotiating a settlement with the Muslims for what the Crusader armies could not win on the battlefield. Frederick obtained control of Jerusalem and Nazareth. In the Sixth Crusade (1248 – 1254 C.E.), Louis IX led an army in an unsuccessful attempt to capture Egypt. Sixteen years later (1270 C.E.) Louis IX died in the Seventh Crusade outside of Tunis. In 1291 C.E., Acre, the last Christian enclave in the Holy Land, fell to the Muslims.

8.2.7 *Consequences of the Crusades*

Except for the First Crusade, the Crusades failed to reach their objective of winning control of the Holy Land. The Crusades, however, had a number of positive consequences. The Crusades brought thousands of Europeans to the Near East. Trade was stimulated and the pace of economic growth increased. Culturally, the Crusaders were overawed with the wealth and accomplishments of both the Byzantine Empire and the Muslim civilization. The Crusades helped renew an interest in the ancient world. The negative effects of the Crusades cannot be ignored. Thousands of Jews and Muslims were massacred and the relations between Europe and the Byzantine Empire collapsed.

8.3   JEWS IN THE MIDDLE AGES

8.3.1 *Jews in the East*

The persecution of Jews which accompanied the Crusades is an important episode in the history of European Jewry. In 135 C.E. the Romans (aftermath of Bar Kochba revolt) prohibited Jews from living in Jerusalem. Many Jews migrated to Babylon. Around 500 C.E. Jewish religious scholars produced the Babylonian Talmud. Under the Sassanids the Jews were persecuted. After the Muslim victory Jews were usually tolerated in Iraq and Persia.

8.3.2   *Jews in Western Europe*

Rome granted citizenship to Jews in 212 C.E. The early Christian emperors (Constantine, Theodosius, and Justinian) issued a series of Jewish decrees which deprived Jews of full citizenship. Pope Gregory I ended (590 – 604 C.E.) the Church's policy of forced baptism and granted Jews the status of defenseless foreigners. Jews were placed under the protection of the various Christian kings. Two centuries later, Charlemagne's son, Louis the Pious, granted Jews certain privileges (including the right to deal in money). The Church prohibited Christians from lending money at interest (usury). Jews became the Empire's financial agents. Urban II's call for the First Crusade in 1095 C.E. opened a period of persecution. The first pogrom against the Jews took place during this period. In 1103 C.E. Henry IV denied Jews the right to bear arms. Since only freemen could bear arms, Henry's proclamation meant that henceforth Jews were considered "unfree." Between 1096 and 1215 C.E. the level and frequency of the persecutions of Jews increased. Jews were accused of blasphemy and ritual murder. In 1215 C.E. the fourth Lateran Council prohibited Jews from holding office and designated certain clothing for Jews to wear as well as areas in which Jews were allowed to live (ghettos). In 1306 C.E. Jews were expelled from France. The outbreak of the Black Death in 1347 C.E. unleashed a wave of pogroms. Three hundred Jewish communities were destroyed in Germany alone. The persecution of Jews reached its high point in Spain between 1391 and 1492 C.E., culminating in Torquemada's expulsion of the Jews from Spain in 1492.

THE JEWISH DIASPORA

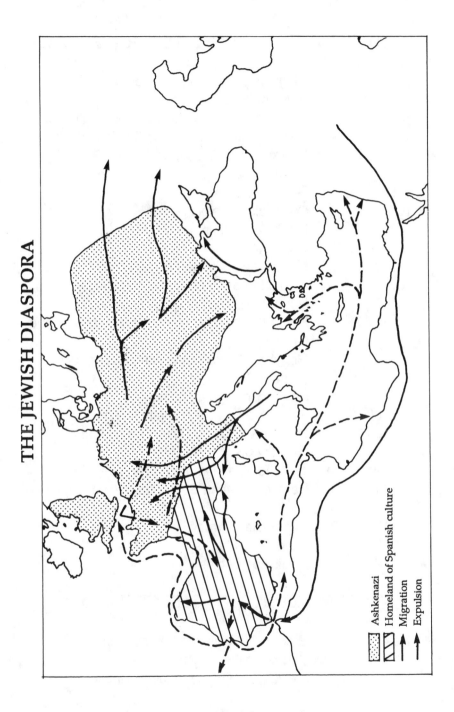

Ashkenazi

Homeland of Spanish culture

Migration

Expulsion

CHRONOLOGY OF THE REFORM PAPACY

910	Cluny inspires reform movement
1040	Pax Dei (Peace of God)
1046	Synod of Sutri; Western emperor calls on Pope Clemens to cleanse the Church
1049 – 1054	Leo X marshalls support for the "Primacy of Peter"
1054	Great Schism
1059	Cardinals will elect pope
	Lay investiture is prohibited
1073 – 1085	Gregory VII
	Monarchical idea of the papacy
1074	Beginning of Investiture Controversy with Henry IV
1076	Henry IV and German bishops depose Pope Gregory
1076	Gregory VII excommunicates Henry IV (Lenten Synod)
1077	Henry comes to Canossa
1080	Henry's second excommunication
1084	Henry crowns anti-Pope Clemens III
1085	Gregory dies
12th and 13th	centuries—period of universal papal rule
1167	Heretical Cathari Sect (dualistic conception of God)
1200 –1229	Albigensian heresy
1210	Waldensian heresy
1215	Inquisition begins

CHRONOLOGY OF THE CRUSADES

1074	Gregory VII calls for the liberation of the Church of the Holy Sepulcher
1095	Alexius Comnenus requests aid from pope

	Urban II to fight the Seljuk Turks
1095	November 26, Urban II calls for a Crusade in the sermon *Deus Io Volt* (God Wills It) at Clermont
1096 – 1099	First Crusade
1099	Jerusalem captured July 15 Kingdom of Jerusalem established under Godfrey of Bouillon (1099 – 1187)
1147 – 1149	Fall of Edessa led to Second Crusade Conrad III fails to conquer Damascus
1187	Salidin captures Jerusalem, ending kingdom of Jerusalem
1189 – 1192	Third Crusade; Frederick Barbarossa drowned; Richard the Lionhearted negotiated armistice with Saladin; Pilgrims allowed to visit Jerusalem
1202 – 1204	Fourth Crusade; Pope Innocent III sends Crusader army against Egypt ; Venetians use Crusaders to loot Constantinople
1212	Children's Crusade; thousands of children transported from Marseilles to Alexandria and sold into slavery
1228 – 1229	Fifth Crusade; Frederick II excommunicated. Obtained Jerusalem by treaty from Sultan El Kamil of Egypt
1248 – 1254	Sixth Crusade; Saint Louis (Louis IX) tries to capture Egypt
1270	Seventh Crusade; Saint Louis dies in effort to win Tunis
1291	Acre falls; Last Christian enclave in the Holy Land is lost

CHRONOLOGY OF THE JEWS
IN THE MIDDLE AGES

132-135	Jews prohibited from entering Jerusalem after failure of revolt at Bar Kochba
212	Romans grant Jews citizenship
300 – 500	Jewish Decrees of Christian emperors strip Jews of many of their rights (Constantine ca. 320, Thedosius 417 and 423, and Justinian)
ca. 500	Jews persecuted under Sassanids Babylonian Talmud
590 – 604	Gregory the Great ended forced baptism Jews to be considered defenseless foreigners under personal protection of kings
814 – 840	Louis the Pious (Charlemagne's son) grants privileges including the right to deal in money
1096 – 1099	First Crusade Pogroms led by Peter the Hermit
1215	4th Lateran Council prohibited Jews from holding public office Designated certain apparel
1236	Frederick II declared the "bondage of the Jews"
1306 – 1354	Jews expelled from France
1347 – 1354	Black Death 3500 Jewish communities destroyed in Germany
1391 – 1492	Persecution of Jews in Spain
1492	Torquemada expels Jews from Spain
1496	Jews expelled from Portugal

CHAPTER 9

CULTURE IN THE HIGH MIDDLE AGES

9.1 THE REVIVAL OF LEARNING

Europeans displayed phenomenal intellectual and cultural vitality in the period between 1050 and 1300 C.E. During the early Middle Ages the majority of Europeans were illiterate. Towards the middle of the eleventh century there were signs of a cultural revival. These changes did not touch the lives of most Europeans. Probably more than ninety percent of the population continued to live on the land. The intellectual climate, however, was improving. By 1100 C.E. the Magyar, Muslim, and Viking threat to Europe had passed. The growth in commerce between East and West offered Europeans contact with the Islamic and Byzantine civilizations. New cities and towns presented an opportunity for intellectuals to gather. The cultural awakening of the high Middle Ages affected only a small number of intellectuals. Nevertheless, the advances in education, philosophy, science, literature, and the arts that unfolded during this period had long-range consequences.

9.1.1 *Education in the Early Middle Ages*

During the early Middle Ages monasteries served as schools and repositories for knowledge of antiquity. Monks produced copies of ancient manuscripts as part of their daily work. Other monks taught in monastical schools. These schools existed in order to provide new members of the clergy. Some monastical schools permitted a small number of non-clerical students to attend.

9.1.2 *Charlemagne's Educational Reforms*

Charlemagne initiated a number of educational reforms. He mandated that bishops open schools at each cathedral. Charlemagne went so far as to found a palace school for his family and court. He invited Alcuin of York (England) to come to Aix-la-Chapelle to reorganize the Empire's educational affairs. The evidence that has survived from the tenth and eleventh centuries supports the conclusion that many bishops ignored Charlemagne's reforms.

9.1.3 *Cathedral Schools*

After 1000 C.E. monastery schools restricted admission to only those who were pursuing lives within the Church. The expansion of trade and the need for clerks and government officials who could read and write stimulated a demand for a new kind of school. In 1179 C.E. cathedrals were required to set aside sufficient revenue to support one teacher.

9.1.4 *The Appearance of Universities*

Universities were an outgrowth of the revival of learning. The word *university* derives from the Latin word "universitas," which means "guild." The first universities were corporations of students and teachers modeled on medieval guilds. Italian students organized the earliest universities in Bologna (law) and Salerno (medicine). Philip Augustus granted the faculty and students of the cathedral school in Paris privileged status in 1200 C.E. In 1231 C.E. Pope Gregory IX acknowledged the importance of the University of Paris in a papal decree. The early universities had a distinctive character. Parisians called the area around the University of Paris the "Latin Quarter" because Latin was spoken by the students and their teachers. Professors required students seeking a master's degree to write a "masterpiece" in the same way that apprentices who wished to become masters of their craft had to produce a "master" work. Town-and-gown relations were often stormy. Civil authorities regularly censured students for their riotous behavior. In 1209 C.E. the chancellor of Cambridge University ordered the school closed because of student disturbances. Those who studied in the medieval universities did not, however, spend their time in frivolous pursuits. The medieval universities were the focal point of the intellectual revival that found its best expression in men like Thomas Aquinas and Roger Bacon.

9.2   SCHOLASTICISM

The dominant philosophical, scientific, and theological tendencies of the high Middle Ages can be grouped together under the term scholasticism. Scholasticism was a way of viewing the world and man's relationship with providence. As such, scholasticism was both a method of teaching and approaching questions and a specific content. Scholasticism arose out of the efforts of European intellectuals to reconcile reason and faith. The increased contact with the Byzantine Empire and the Islamic world raised a number of questions about how a Christian should make sense of the pagan tradition. During the early Middle Ages Tertullian had spoken for the majority of his contemporaries when he declared "I believe because it is absurd" (Latin: *credo quia absurdum*). After 1050 C.E. Europeans in-

91

creasingly sought to find ways to accommodate reason and faith. In this process the high Middle Ages produced its greatest theological and philosophical work.

9.2.1 St. Anselm

The Benedictine monk, St. Anselm (1033 – 1109 C.E.), hoped to harmonize faith and reason. His goal was "faith seeking to understand." Anselm believed that there was no conflict separating man's spiritual and rational natures. Both were part of God's gifts to human beings. Anselm joined reason and faith when he proclaimed his personal credo "I believe in order to understand."

9.2.2 Peter Abelard

The French priest, Peter Abelard (1079 – 1142 C.E.), was a far more controversial proponent of the marriage of reason and faith. Abelard won notoriety for his spirited lectures at the cathedral school of Notre Dame (the nucleus of the University of Paris). Abelard's disastrous love affair with Heloise (niece of Fulbert, canon of Notre Dame) is recorded in the lovers' letters. When Fulbert discovered the affair he placed Heloise in a nunnery and ordered his servants to castrate Abelard. Abelard later produced an autobiography, *The Story of My Calamities*, that chronicled his tumultuous life. In *Sic et Non (Yes and No)*, Abelard collected statements in the Bible and by Church leaders which contradicted one another. Some of Abelard's contemporaries accused him of undermining the Church's authority in this book. Abelard's intention, however, was just the opposite. He believed that reason could resolve the apparent contradictions between the two authorities. Bernard of Clairvaux forced Abelard to retire from public debate. The Church judged Abelard's views heretical.

9.2.3 *Thomas Aquinas*

Scholasticism reached its zenith in the life and work of Thomas Aquinas (1225 – 1274 C.E.). Born in Naples and educated in Paris, Aquinas was a Dominican who never tired in his effort to prove faith and reason could be reconciled. He believed that there were two orders of truth. On one level, reason could demonstrate propositions such as the existence of God. On a higher level, some things such as the nature of the Trinity must be accepted on faith. Aquinas based his scholasticism on a conception of the universe as a great chain of being. An omniscient, omnipotent God had called everything to being. Each part of creation had its place in an order which stretched from inanimate matter to God. Man occupied a place midway between the material and the spiritual. Reason gave human beings the power to understand some things. God's mysteries were matters of faith. Aquinas collected his reflections in two great works: *The Summa contra Gentiles* and the *Summa Theologica*. The Church canonized Aquinas shortly after his death in 1274 C.E.

9.3 SCIENCE AND SCHOLASTICISM

9.3.1 *The Rediscovery of Aristotle*

Aquinas's effort to reconcile faith and reason was not without its critics. The Bishop of Paris condemned 219 of Aquinas's teachings four years after the philosopher's death. Aquinas's critics attacked him because of his dependence on Aristotle. They claimed that he had Christianized the pagan Aristotle.

9.3.2 *Albert Magnus*

Albert Magnus (1206 – 1280 C.E.) exercised an important influence on Aquinas and the development of scholasticism. Magnus, a German Dominican, was Aquinas's teacher in Paris, where he spent most of his life. Magnus attempted to join Augustine to Aristotle. Magnus advocated the use of empirical research guided by observation and testing.

9.3.3 *Grosseteste and Bacon*

Robert Grosseteste (1175 – 1253 C.E.) and his student, Roger Bacon (ca. 1214 – 1294 C.E.), were the two most influential English philosophers and scientists in the high Middle Ages. Grosseteste, chancellor of Oxford University, was one of the first Europeans to translate works directly from Greek. Until the thirteenth century the Hellenistic tradition had passed from Greek into Syriac and, then, after 750 C.E. from Syriac into Arabic. Western scholars began to translate these works into Latin in the twelfth century. Grosseteste's work opened a new perspective on antiquity. Grosseteste was an Aristotelian who tried to demonstrate that the world was round. He performed experiments on the refraction of light and demanded that his students ground their speculations in observation and experiment. Roger Bacon has eclipsed his teacher's fame because of his knack for showing a theory's practical implications. Bacon anticipated the invention of the telescope. He stressed the importance of mathematics, and argued that observation should guide reason. The teachers and students of the medieval universities were not scientists in the modern sense. Nonetheless, men like Grosseteste and Bacon did encourage observation. They never questioned the assumption on which scholasticism rested: that faith and reason were in harmony.

9.3.4 *Medicine*

The increase in the contact between East and West during the high Middle Ages led to advances in Western medicine. The University of Salerno (southern Italy) became a center of medical studies in the twelfth and thirteenth centuries. The appearance of a university in Salerno is partly explained by Sicily's proximity. The professors and students in Salerno had access to an area that had been under both Byzantine and Muslim rulers.

9.4 SCHOLASTICISM AND THE LAW

9.4.1 *Secular Law*

Scholasticism penetrated into every aspect of intellectual life in the high Middle Ages. The development of legal studies in the twelfth and thirteenth centuries illustrates how far-reaching its consequences were for society. Until the eleventh century, law in the West had consisted of the customs of the various European peoples. Irnerius (1088 – 1125 C.E.), a scholar at the University of Bologna, introduced Justinian's *Corpus Juris Civilis* to the West. Irnerius was the first in a series of Western legal scholars who undertook to place legal studies on a universally valid footing.

9.4.2 *Canon Law*

In 1140 C.E. Gratian, a monk in Bologna, published a *Concordance of Discordant Canons*. This was the beginning of the Church's struggle to reform Canon Law (laws governing the Church). Gratian collected passages in the Bible which appeared to contradict papal declarations. One of Abelard's students, Peter Lombard, carried Gratian's procedures even further. Between 1155 and 1157 C.E. Lombard collected many examples of contradictory statements within the canonical tradition. He published his researches in his *Book of Sentences*. Lombard employed reason and faith in assessing each statement. He drew out the statement's consequences and reached a conclusion as to its correctness.

9.5   LITERATURE AND MUSIC

The literary production of the high Middle Ages can be divided into two groups. At the universities, Latin continued to be the language which intellectuals used. Groups of secular poets such as the Golliards composed satirical poems and burlesques in Latin. The origin of the name "Golliard" is uncertain. One tradition maintains that the name arose out of a reference to the devil because the Golliards often wrote satires on religious themes.

9.5.1   *Vernacular Literature*

The most vibrant literary works were written in vernacular languages. New subject matter was explored and new genres appeared.

The Chansons de Geste. The Chansons de Geste refer to the long epic poems (composed between 1050 – 1150 C.E.). These poems were sometimes anonymous and were part of an oral tradition. The *Song of Roland* (chronicled the betrayal of one of Charlemagne's warriors as he returned from Spain), the *Song of the Nibelungs* (story of the German hero Siegfried), the Icelandic *Eddas*, and *Song of the Cid* are among the best representatives of this genre.

The Troubadours. A tradition of lyrical poetry developed in southern France in the twelfth century. The troubadour poets composed their love poems in Provencal (a language related to modern French). The troubadour poetry treated themes involving love, warfare, and current political affairs. In Germany an indigenous lyrical poetic tradition called the Minnesingers flourished in the twelfth and thirteenth centuries.

Romances and Fabliaux. Chretien de Troyes (1165 – 1190 C.E.) helped create the genre of the romance. Chretien de Troyes built a long story around the life of the legendary (sixth century) English King Arthur. In Germany, Wolfram von Eschenbach used the story of the quest for the Holy Grail as the basis for *Parzival.* Gottfried von Strasbourg used an adulterous love affair for the subject of his *Tristan. The Romance of the Rose* was the most famous of the medieval romances. *The Romance of the Rose* (begun in 1230 C.E. by William Lorris and finished forty years later in 1270 C.E. by John of Meun) illustrates the growing secular tendency of the vernacular tradition. The romances of the late twelfth and thirteenth centuries had a direct influence on the later development of the novel as a literary form. The short *fabliaux* represented the opposite extreme. The poets who created the *fabliaux* belonged to a verse tradition that goes back to Aesop. These poems evolved into short stories. Many of the *fabliaux* ridiculed the clergy (monks in particular) for violating their sacred vows. Boccaccio (1313 – 1375 C.E.) and Chaucer (1340 – 1400 C.E. belong to this tradition.

Dante. Dante (1265 – 1321 C.E.) was the greatest medieval poet. Born in Florence, Dante played an active role in the city's political affairs until his exile at the beginning of the fourteenth century. This disaster became the occasion for Dante's *Commedia (Divine Comedy).* In 100 cantos, Dante poet tells the story of Dante pilgrim's journey through the Inferno, progress up the Mount of Purgatory, and, finally, ascension through the celestial spheres to God's abode. Dante's work provides a poetic synthesis of the pagan and Christian traditions. Guided by Virgil and influenced by Lucan, Ovid, and Statius, Dante creates a vision of heaven and hell and man's relation to God while commenting on the political events of his time.

Music. Late in the twelfth century a new conception of harmony appeared. Throughout antiquity and the early Middle

Ages music was homophonic (one melody at a time). In 1170 C.E. a polyphonic (two or more melodies performed at the same time) mass was presented at Notre Dame Cathedral in Paris. The introduction of polyphony opened new possibilities for both secular and religious musical compositions.

9.5.2 *Architecture*

Two major architectural traditions developed in the high Middle Ages. The Romanesque style reached its high point between 1000 and 1150 C.E. The Romanesque style was based on a conception of building which developed the rounded arch, thick stone walls, and tiny windows. After 1150 C.E. the Gothic style came into vogue. The first Gothic church was built at St. Denis (in France) in 1144 C.E. The Gothic architects created buildings that emphasized light. Gothic architects decorated churches and public buildings with rich, ornamental facades. These facades contrasted with their simple interiors. Art historians have characterized them as scholasticism in stone.

CHRONOLOGY OF CULTURAL EVENTS IN THE HIGH MIDDLE AGES

980 – 1037	Avicenna
ca. 1000 – 1200	Romanesque architecture flourishes
1088 – 1125	Irnerius
ca. 1050 – 1150	Chansons de Geste
ca. 1095	*Song of Roland*
1033 – 1109	St. Anselm
1079 – 1142	Peter Abelard
ca. 1100 – 1220	Troubadour poetry
ca. 1120	*Rubaiyat* of Omar Khayyam
1126 – 1198	Averroes, "The Commentator" on Aristotle
1135 – 1204	Moses Maimonides
ca. 1140	Gratian

1148	Anna Comnena's biography of her father
ca. 1150 – 1500	Gothic style flourishes
ca. 1165 – 1190	Poetry of Chretien de Troyes
1168 – 1253	Robert Grosseteste
1179	Cathedral schools required to pay a teacher
ca. 1170	Development of polyphony in Paris
ca. 1180	Windmill appears in Europe
ca. 1100 – 1300	Foundation of first universities
ca. 1200	Wolfram von Eschenbach
1206 – 1280	Albert Magnus
ca.1210	Gottfried von Strassburg
ca. 1214 – 1294	Roger Bacon
1221 – 1274	St. Bonaventure
1231	Gregory IX appoints a commission to "correct" Aristotle
1250 – 1277	Height of scholasticism
b. 1265	Duns Scotus
1225 – 1275	Thomas Aquinas
ca. 1270	*Romance of the Rose*
ca. 1285 – 1349	William of Ockham
ca. 1290	Mechanical clock is invented
ca. 1300 – 1327	Meister Eckhart
1305 – 1337	Giotto
1304 – 1323	Dante's *Commedia*
ca. 1350	Boccaccio's *Decameron*
ca. 1390	Chaucer's *Canterbury Tales*
1300 – 1500	High point of Nominalism
ca. 1450	Printing with movable type
1453	Heavy artillery used by Turks to win Constantinople

CHAPTER 10

THE LATE MIDDLE AGES

10.1 THE CATASTROPHIC 14TH CENTURY

Three centuries of population growth and economic prosperity ended in the fourteenth century. Natural disasters and warfare led to a drastic reduction in population and widespread social unrest. During this period, the Church passed through a wrenching internal crisis that left it permanently scarred. By 1450 C.E. Europe was beginning its recovery.

10.1.1 *Famine*

Population grew rapidly in the high Middle Ages. The improvement in the climate, the opening of new agricultural areas, and the employment of more efficient technologies created an agricultural surplus. By the end of the thirteenth century, there were signs that the population growth had outdistanced available food supplies. Climatologists believe that by 1300 C.E. the climate had cooled and the amount of rainfall increased. In 1290 C.E. there was a widespread famine. After 1300 C.E. famine was a constant threat. Records show that many parts of Europe experienced crop failures in 1309 and

1313 C.E. Torrential rains ruined crops and early frosts destroyed harvests. Historians estimate that between 1315 and 1317 C.E. the population of Europe decreased by as much as 10%. The famines were caused in part by soil exhaustion. Faced with the impossibility of surviving in the countryside, many peasants sought refuge in the already overcrowded towns and cities. Cities were especially vulnerable when shortages occurred. By the midpoint of the fourteenth century malnutrition was endemic.

10.1.2 *The Black Death*

Historians believe that the Black Death, or the Bubonic Plague, broke out in China around 1333 C.E. By 1347 C.E. travelers and merchants had carried the plague over the Silk Route to the Near East and into Messina in Sicily. In 1348 C.E. the plague began to ravage Europe. The general malnutrition meant that Europeans were particularly susceptible to illness and disease. Between 1348 and 1351 C.E. the plague advanced across Europe. Outbreaks of the plague occurred roughly every decade for the next one hundred and fifty years (1362, 1375, etc.). It was not until 1918 C.E. that the plague bacillus was identified. By the end of the fourteenth century, the plague had reduced Europe's population to below its level in 1100 C.E. Some historians estimate that the plague killed between one-half to two-thirds of Europe's population.

10.1.3 *Warfare and Civil Unrest*

The fourteenth century opened a period of warfare which devastated every part of Europe. Between 1337 and 1453 C.E. England and France waged the Hundred Years' War. Wars broke out on the Iberian peninsula, northern Italy, and Eastern Europe. Medieval warfare exacted a heavy toll on non-combatants. Armies lived off the land. Troops destroyed crops as they marched across fields. Armies looted grain stores to feed them-

THE SPREAD OF THE PLAGUE

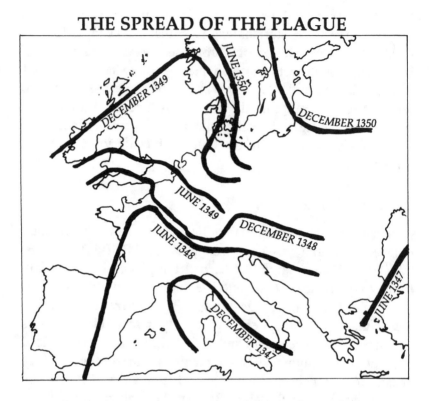

selves. During this period peasants revolted against their masters. After a decade of famine, the free peasants of Flanders revolted when the nobility attempted to impose certain obsolescent manorial duties. The peasants struggled for five years before the nobles suppressed their rebellion. As many as 20,000 French peasants died a few years later, in 1358, in a similar revolt. Called the Jacquerie, the French peasants, like their Flemish counterparts, were protesting against the nobles' attempt to introduce antiquated taxes and duties. The English Peasants' Revolt in 1381 C.E. was the largest rebellion in English history. English peasants rebelled when the government passed laws which would bind the peasants to the land and create a new set of taxes. The Flemish and French peasants revolted when conditions were worsening. The English peasants rebelled because things were getting better. The plague and the continuous state of warfare had created a labor shortage. All of these revolts failed. Civil disorders were not restricted to the countryside. Wage laborers in Florence (1378 C.E.), textile workers in Ghent (1382 C.E.), and the Parisian poor rose up against the well-to-do.

10.1.4 *The Economic and Financial Crisis*

During the high Middle Ages an economy based on subsistence agriculture was transformed into an economy in which traders and bankers played an increasingly important role. The crop failures, warfare, plague, and domestic unrest combined to produce an economic crisis. In 1339 C.E. the banks (the word "bank" comes from the Latin word "bancus" which refers to the bank or bench where bankers or judges do their business) collapsed. In 1343 and 1346 C.E. the Florentine Peruzzie and Bardi banking families went bankrupt. The collapse of these and other banks was paralleled by a general currency devaluation. In the thirteenth century the Byzantine gold *solidus*, the Venetian *ducat*, and the Florentine *florin* had served as the basis of international trade and finance. By the close of the fourteenth century all three had lost their value. This economic and financial crisis meant that Europe returned to its pre-1100 C.E. level of economic development. Economic historians estimate that it took 150 years (until ca. 1500 C.E.) for Europe to reach the level of economic production of 1340 C.E.

10.2 SUMMARY OF POLITICAL DEVELOPMENTS IN THE LATE MIDDLE AGES

10.2.1 *The Concept of Europe*

Before the thirteenth century the word "Europe" (Latin "Europa") was not in general usage. Christendom (Latin "Christianitas") was the term used in the West. By 1500 C.E. the word "Europe" had replaced "Christendom." This shift in terminology from a religious conception to a term that has a geographical and cultural significance developed as the external threats to Europe receded and the internal rivalry between the Christians grew. In the Middle Ages there was one Christendom. The early modern period begins with the outbreak of a struggle between the different European states for hegemony over their fellow Christians and infidels.

10.2.2 *Germany and the Empire*

Frederick II's death in 1250 C.E. ended the Hohenstaufen Dynasty. The period between Frederick's death and Rudolf of Hapsburg's coronation (1273 C.E.) as Emperor is called the Great Interregnum. The other powerful German princes used the Hohenstaufens' demise as an opportunity to redistribute their lands. These nobles developed a system of selecting the emperor through an electoral process. The king of Bohemia, Ottakar, challenged Rudolf of Hapsburg's imperial authority. In 1278 C.E. Rudolf's forces defeated the Bohemians in the Battle of Marchfeld. The "German Lands" (as the Empire came to be known) were more prosperous than England and France in the fifteenth century. Politically, the existence of a number of powerful nobles and principalities meant that the Empire was condemned to fragmentation at a time when England and France were laying the groundwork for strong national monarchies.

10.2.3 *The Hundred Years' War*

The Hundred Years' War began out of the rivalry between two medieval princes and ended in a war between two nation states. The death of Charles IV (last Capetian king) precipitated a crisis over who would be his successor. Philip VI of the Valois family was chosen king over the protests of Edward III of England who claimed to be the rightful heir. Edward's mother was Charles IV's daughter. Edward's control of Normandy and his strong position in Gascony and Brittany made his claim that much stronger. Fighting broke out in 1337 C.E. and continued until 1453 C.E. With a population of fifteen million as compared to England's four million, France should have had no difficulty in defeating England. The English, however, defeated the French in the war's major battles (Crecy, 1346 C.E.; Poitiers, 1356 C.E.; and Agincourt, 1415 C.E.). Armed with long bows and hungry for plunder, the English infantry defeated the French soldiers. The Duke of Burgundy's defection from the French side in 1414 C.E. made it appear that France was on the edge of collapse. In 1429 C.E. a peasant girl named Joan of Arc announced that she had received a visitation from God. God, she said, had commanded her to come to the aid of Charles VIII (the uncrowned French King). Charles gave her command of his troops. Joan succeeded in driving the English out of most of central France. The Burgundians captured Joan in 1430 C.E. The English accused her of being a witch. She was tried and condemned to death in 1431 C.E. Four years later Burgundy broke with England. In 1453 C.E. the French drove the English out of Bordeaux. England was left with only the port of Calais and the Channel Islands. In 1588 the French captured Calais.

10.2.4 *The Formation of the Russian Empire*

The Mongol invasions cut Russia off from the West in the thirteenth century. In 1328 C.E. the metropolitan (head of the Russian Orthodox Church) moved his residence to the principality of Muscovy. The Byzantine Empire exerted less influence on Muscovy's development than on Kievian Russia. In 1462 C.E. Ivan III used the collapse of the Mongol Empire as an opportunity to expand Muscovy's influence. In 1472 C.E. Ivan married the daughter of the last Byzantine Emperor. Ivan adopted the Byzantine double-headed eagle as the symbol for his state and took the title Tsar (from Caesar). In 1492 C.E.

Ivan proclaimed that Moscow was the "New Constantinople." Five years later a monk named Philotheus declared that Russia was the "Third Rome."

10.3 THE DECLINE OF THE CHURCH

10.3.1 *The Babylonian Captivity*

Pope Boniface VIII (1294 – 1303 C.E.) opened the fourteenth century with the bold assertion of the pope's supremacy (Papal Bull "Unam Sanctum"). In 1303 C.E. agents of Philip IV (whom Boniface had excommunicated) took the pope prisoner. In 1305 C.E. Clement V (formerly archbishop of Bordeaux) became pope (1305 – 1314 C.E.). In 1309 C.E. Clement moved from Rome to Avignon in southern France. Historians refer to the period from 1309 to 1377 C.E. as the Babylonian Captivity. During this period all the popes were French. The sumptuous accommodations at Avignon and the popes' subservience to the French king fueled the growing antipapal sentiments throughout Europe. St. Catherine of Siena appealed to Pope Gregory XI to return to Rome. He agreed and returned in 1378.

10.3.2 *The Great Schism*

Gregory's return to Rome precipitated a crisis. When he died, two groups of cardinals met to elect his successor. One body met in Rome, the other in Avignon. Each elected a pope: Urban VI in Rome and Clement VII in Avignon. Between 1378 and 1417 C.E. Latin Christendom was divided into two camps. Proponents of the Conciliar Theory (that Councils of the Church had the power to resolve doctrinal disputes) gained new supporters. In 1409 C.E. the Council of Pisa tried to resolve the Great Schism. They declared Peter's throne vacant and elected a new pope. This produced an intolerable situation in which there were three popes. Between 1414 and 1417 C.E. thirty-three cardinals, nine hundred bishops, and more than two thousand doctors of theology met in Constance. The Council of Constance proclaimed the Church's unity and deposed all of the current popes. The Council elected Martin V the new pope. The Council struck against heresy and ordered John Hus and Hieronymus of Prague to be burned at the stake. The Conciliar Movement succeeded in resolving the Great Schism. It failed in achieving the needed internal reforms. One result of this failure to achieve reform was that the pope's secular power was increased and the tendency of the Church to divide into national churches grew.

10.3.3 Heretical Movements

The Flagellants. The calamities of the fourteenth century produced a variety of new forms of religious expression. After 1331 C.E. there were many reports of flagellation being performed as a religious ritual. The flagellants believed that by whipping themselves they could lessen God's wrath. The plague's outbreak intensified the movement.

Mysticism. The inward, contemplative way of mysticism represented the opposite extreme to the flagellants. A German Dominican, Meister Eckhart (ca. 1260 – 1327 C.E.), was one of the leaders of this movement. Eckhart preached that each individual possessed a "spark" of God within his or her soul. Attendance at church was of secondary importance to the cultivation of the inner way to God. In the fifteenth century the mystical movement found its clearest expression in Thomas à Kempis's *Imitation of Christ* (1427 C.E.).

John Wycliffe and the Lollards. The Oxford theologian John Wycliffe (ca. 1330 – 1384) criticized the Church for its corruption. Wycliffe was a firm Augustinian and believed in predestination. He advised his supporters (called Lollards) to avoid contact with corrupt priests. The Church declared

Wycliffe's teachings heretical after his death. In 1414 C.E. the Lollards failed in their attempt to oust corrupt Church officials; they were driven underground and Wycliffe's movement failed. Wycliffe helped prepare the way for the Protestant Reformation a century later.

John Hus. John Wycliffe's ideas reached Bohemia (modern Czechoslovakia) in the early fifteenth century. John Hus (1337 – 1415 C.E.) used Wycliffe's teachings as the basis for his attack on the Church. His sermons generated widespread support. In 1414 C.E. he was summoned to the Council of Constance to defend his beliefs. The Council granted him free passage and promised that he would not be harmed. When Hus arrived in Constance the Council reneged on its promise and tried Hus as a heretic. He was convicted and burned. Hus's supporters in Bohemia rebelled. Led by John Zizka, the Hussite armies defeated several groups of "crusading" knights that the Church dispatched from Germany. Bohemia did not return to the Catholic fold until the Catholic Counter-Reformation.

10.4   THE BREAKDOWN OF THE MEDIEVAL WORLD VIEW

10.4.1 *Scholasticism in the Late Middle Ages*

William of Ockham. Scholasticism underwent a fundamental change in the late Middle Ages. Aquinas had argued that reason could be used to prove much of revelation. Many of the philosophers and theologians in the fourteenth and fifteenth centuries abandoned this position. Duns Scotus (1265 – 1308 C.E.), an English philosopher, argued that reason cannot prove the essential articles of the Christian faith. Duns Scotus's student, William of Ockham (ca. 1285 – 1349 C.E.) was the most radical proponent of the "modernist" position. Ockham's outlook was known as Nominalism. Nominalists distinguished between that which can be demonstrated by human reason and the unprovable articles of faith. In practice, nominalists argued that only individual things were real. Collectivities were fictions created by grouping things together and giving them names. Ockham's nominalism encouraged an empirical outlook.

Nicholaus of Cusa. Nicholaus of Cusa's work (1401 – 1464 C.E.) embodied the discontent of many of his contemporaries with scholasticism. Cusa argued that the universe had no center and that its plan could not be understood rationally. In his major work *Of Learned Ignorance* (1440 C.E.), Cusa contended that every religion illustrated part of God's Divine truth. To Cusa, God is that entity which resolves all contradictions.

10.4.2 *Literature*

The Nominalists' interest in individual things was reflected in the development of naturalism in literature. Naturalism may be defined as the effort to represent events and individual things as they are. The naturalist writers of the fourteenth and fifteenth centuries did not abandon religious themes. They depicted their subject matter, however, with a skepticism and irony not present in the high Middle Ages.

Boccaccio. The Italian Giovanni Boccaccio's (1313 – 1375 C.E.) *Decameron* (written between 1348 and 1351 C.E.) portrayed the efforts of seven young ladies and three young men to escape the ravages of plague. The ten agreed to entertain one another by telling stories. The stories depicted people as they were and not as they might have wished to be. The *Decameron*'s brisk pace and humorous tone make it appear modern.

Chaucer. Geoffrey Chaucer's (ca. 1340 – 1400 C.E.) incomplete *Canterbury Tales* is also a collection of stories. Chaucer's characters are pilgrims on their way to Canterbury. As presented by Chaucer, they are recognizably human in their appetites and affectations.

10.4.3 *Naturalism in Art*

The new interest in showing things as they really were influenced fourteenth and fifteenth century artists. Giotto (ca. 1267 – 1337 C.E.) refined the art of painting on walls (called frescos because the paint was applied to wet plaster). His paintings of the death of St. Francis and of Christ's wounds brought a new realism to religious art. Giotto's innovations were not limited to the content of his works. Giotto pioneered the use of perspective in his paintings. Northern artists, such as the brothers Hubert and Jan van Eyck (ca. 1366 – 1426, ca. 1380 – 1441 C.E.), and Roger van der Weyden, developed the technique of oil painting. Oil gave them the ability to produce brilliantly colored works that were filled with minute details.

10.4.4 *Technology in the Late Middle Ages*

The late Middle Ages produced a number of revolutionary technical advances. The invention of artillery and the introduction of guns transformed warfare. The heavily armored knight became vulnerable to a peasant with a gun. Artillery made fortified castles obsolete. Improvements in optical devices and navigational instruments allowed Europeans to begin exploring the world. The mechanical clock was another important invention of this period. The first mechanical clocks appeared around 1300 C.E. Dante makes reference to them in the *Divine Comedy*. Mechanical clocks brought a new sense of time. During antiquity and the Middle Ages time followed the rhythm of the seasons. The mechanical clock made possible the precise calculation of events and provided a means by which every facet of life could be regulated. Finally, the invention of printing produced a revolution in human knowledge. Paper replaced parchment as a writing material between 1200 and 1400 C.E. The use of printing presses with paper reduced the cost of books tremendously. This opened up the possibility that Europeans could read books and disseminate their ideas with relative ease. Without the invention of printing, it is difficult to believe that the rebirth of interest in antiquity, which we call the Renaissance, could have occurred at such a rapid pace.

10.5 THE END OF THE MIDDLE AGES

The Middle Ages did not have a precise beginning or fixed end. By 1500 C.E. new forces were transforming Europe. Nation states were forming and capitalism was advancing. The medieval moral economy was being replaced by what moderns would later call the cash nexus. New worlds were being explored. Christianity was in the midst of a crisis. Intellectuals were rediscovering the works of the Greeks and Romans. The calamities of the fourteenth century proved to be the death knell of the medieval world. By 1500 C.E. Europe had entered a new age.

CHRONOLOGY OF
THE LATE MIDDLE AGES

ca. 1300 – 1500	European wide depression
1305 – 1378	Pope Clement V moves to Avignon
	Beginning of Babylonian Captivity
1315 – 1317	Famine and floods
ca. 1330s	Peasant uprisings
ca. 1330 – 1384	John Wycliffe
1337 – 1415	John Hus
1337 – 1453	Hundred Years' War
1343 – 1346	Bank failures in Florence
1348 – 1351	Black Death
1358	Jacquerie, French Peasant Revolt
1378 – 1417	Great Schism
1381	English Peasants' Revolt
1401 – 1464	Nicholaus of Cusa

1414 – 1418	Council of Constance
ca. 1427	*Imitation of Christ*
1431 – 1449	Council of Basel, Defeat of Conciliarism
1492	Ivan III of Muscovy proclaims Moscow the "new Constantinople"
	Expulsion of Jews from Spain
	Columbus